Training and Development Express

Roger Cartwright

- Fast-track route to effective training and development within organizations. Will help maximize the value from the skills and experience of your workforce

- Covers the strategic role training and development plays within organizations. Looks at the differences and similarities of training, development, education, coaching and mentoring. The importance of intellectual capital as a key organizational resource is also explored

- Case studies of TCM.com inc (Canada), British Airways, Unipart (UK), The training component of the US Liberty Ship program during World War 2 and Canon (Japan)

- Includes a comprehensive resources guide, key concepts and thinkers, a 10-step action plan for implementing a training and development programme, and a section of FAQs

>>EXPRESS EXEC.COM<<
essential management thinking at your fingertips

Copyright © Capstone Publishing, 2003

The right of Roger Cartwright to be identified as the author of this book has been asserted in accordance with the Copyright, Designs and Patents Act 1988

First Published 2003 by
Capstone Publishing Limited (a Wiley company)
8 Newtec Place
Magdalen Road
Oxford OX4 1RE
United Kingdom
http://www.capstoneideas.com

CIP catalogue records for this book are available from the British Library and the US Library of Congress

ISBN 1-84112-442-7

Printed and bound in Great Britain by CPI Antony Rowe, Eastbourne

Wiley also publishes its books in a variety of electronic formats. Some content that appears in print may not be available in electronic books.

Websites often change their contents and addresses; details of sites listed in this book were accurate at the time of writing, but may change.

Substantial discounts on bulk quantities of Capstone Books are available to corporations, professional associations and other organizations. For details telephone Capstone Publishing on (+44-1865-798623), fax (+44-1865-240941) or email (info@wiley-capstone.co.uk).

Contents

Introduction to ExpressExec   v

11.01.01 Introduction   1
11.01.02 What is Meant by Training and Development?   5
11.01.03 The Evolution of Training and Development   13
11.01.04 The E-Dimension of Training and Development   25
11.01.05 The Global Dimension of Training and
         Development   35
11.01.06 The State of the Art   47
11.01.07 Training and Development Success Stories   69
11.01.08 Key Concepts and Thinkers   85
11.01.09 Resources for Training and Development   95
11.01.10 Ten Steps to Effective Training and
         Development   105

Frequently Asked Questions (FAQs)   111
Index   115

Introduction to ExpressExec

ExpressExec is a completely up-to-date resource of current business practice, accessible in a number of ways – anytime, anyplace, anywhere. ExpressExec combines best practice cases, key ideas, action points, glossaries, further reading, and resources.

Each module contains 10 individual titles that cover all the key aspects of global business practice. Written by leading experts in their field, the knowledge imparted provides executives with the tools and skills to increase their personal and business effectiveness, benefiting both employee and employer.

ExpressExec is available in a number of formats:

- » **Print** – 120 titles available through retailers or printed on demand using any combination of the 1200 chapters available.
- » **E-Books** – e-books can be individually downloaded from Express-Exec.com or online retailers onto PCs, handheld computers, and e-readers.
- » **Online** – http://www.expressexec.wiley.com/ provides fully searchable access to the complete ExpressExec resource via the Internet – a cost-effective online tool to increase business expertise across a whole organization.

» **ExpressExec Performance Support Solution (EEPSS)** – a software solution that integrates ExpressExec content with interactive tools to provide organizations with a complete internal management development solution.
» **ExpressExec Rights and Syndication** – ExpressExec content can be licensed for translation or display within intranets or on Internet sites.

To find out more visit www.ExpressExec.com or contact elound@wiley-capstone.co.uk.

Introduction

The chapter considers:

» the opposing organizational standpoints with regard to training and development – the concept that training and development is seen as either a cost or an investment;
» the importance of training and development as a motivator; and
» that training and development effectiveness is measured by outcomes rather than inputs.

Manager: "I can't afford to train my staff."
Competitor: "In that case I can't afford not to train mine."

STANDPOINTS

There are two organizational standpoints that can be adopted when considering training and development:

» training and development is a cost the organization needs to bear; or
» training and development is an investment the organization needs to make.

The first approach leads to training and development being regarded as a "grudge purchase" along with insurance and security. In such organizations the outlay of resources (money, time, etc.) on training and development will be resented. It is not only those whose budgets have to pay for training activities that will become resentful as their feelings will percolate down to those being trained and developed. Training and development may be perceived as a waste of time and effort by those it should be helping.

The second approach – training and development as an investment – is much more holistic. Whatever field of activity the organization is in, training and development is an activity that will give the organization a competitive advantage. This is not only because the employees may actually be better at their allotted tasks than those with less training, but also because the employees will be better motivated. In an organization that sees training and development as an investment, employees soon realize that the investment the organization makes in training and developing them also enhances the "saleability" of that employee. An investment in training and development is also an investment in the person being trained and developed.

Frederick Herzberg, whose work on the motivation of managers has become a standard, showed that recognition and achievement were two of the most effective motivators. An organization that invests in training and development is not only recognizing the abilities of its workforce but is also providing achievement opportunities for them.

EFFECTIVE TRAINING AND DEVELOPMENT

Subsequent chapters will stress the point that training and development needs to be structured, planned, and targeted for it to be effective. Effective training and development occurs when both the needs of the organization and the individual being trained and developed are met. Input measures such as how much time, money and so forth have been devoted to training and development provide little or no indication as to the effectiveness of the process. The most important measurements are output related: How have the organization and the individual benefited from the training and development, and how has this increased the organization's (and the individual's) competitive advantage?

Organizations exist to do something, whether it is to manufacture a product or to deliver a service. Training and development is an activity that supports the overall organizational objectives. This is why it is an investment and not a cost that must be borne grudgingly.

Within any study of training and development a series of terms reoccur:

» *learning*
» *training*
» *development*
» *education*
» *coaching*
» *mentoring*.

How these are defined, how they are related, and how they can be used to gain competitive advantage are important issues addressed in this book. It takes a broad view of the training and development process. Other titles in this series look at particular training and development issues in detail.

What is Meant by Training and Development?

The chapter examines the following concepts:

» intellectual capital as an intangible asset;
» learning and the learning curve;
» training to gain and improve skills;
» development as a long-term process that not only provides skills but also changes attitudes;
» education as a social process that transmits societal norms to individuals; and
» individual attention through coaching and mentoring.

INTANGIBLE ASSETS

Organizations typically measure their assets in tangible terms – stock, buildings, investments, cash, etc. However, in addition to these there are intangible assets that may have a value far in excess of the more tangible assets.

Consider what Mickey Mouse is worth to Disney or what a gifted program writer is worth to Microsoft. The value may be impossible to calculate in absolute terms, but it is likely to be many times the conventional worth of either asset.

Andrew Mayo[1] has divided intangible assets into three main groups:

» *customer capital* – the value of brands and reputation, and the relationship the customer feels he or she has with the organization;
» *structural capital* – the value of patents, organizational know-how, and culture; and
» *human capital* – the value of the experience, loyalty, knowledge, and attributes of the employees.

Together these categories comprise the "intellectual capital" of the organization. The most important component is that of human capital.

The worth of intellectual capital was graphically illustrated by an incident recounted by Clive Irving[2] in 1993. He tells how at a meeting between Boeing and Soviet aeronautical engineers during the development of the Boeing 747 "jumbo" jet, the Soviets made a number of offers (eventually offering $10mn) for a copy of the company's *Design Objectives and Criteria*. A dull title perhaps, but it contained the sum of Boeing's knowledge about jet airliner design from the 707 onwards. Boeing took the offer seriously enough to institute extra security procedures to protect the company's hard-won knowledge.

When Philip Morris purchased Kraft for $12.6bn in 1988, the paper worth of the company was about $2.1bn and the value of the brand $10.5bn – so they paid six times the paper worth to acquire the name. Put another way, the intangible asset (the brand name) was valued at six times the tangible assets of the company.

DEFINITIONS

Training and development is the means by which an organization invests in its employees. Change requires new skills and attitudes, so organizations that do not invest in training and development cannot hope to benefit from change – indeed they may well not survive change.

As mentioned in the previous chapter, within any study of training and development there are a series of terms that reoccur: learning; training; development; education; coaching; and mentoring.

Learning

Learning is the process by which behavior and attitudes are changed. One of the major debates in child development and education has been on the question of how much behavior is innate and how much is learnt – the nature versus nurture debate.

A psychological definition of learning[3] is:

"any change in the general activity of an organism the effects of which persist and recur over a period of time and which are strengthened by repetition and practice."

Although this is quite an old definition, it covers the major points about learning very comprehensively – the fact that learning persists and recurs and that it is strengthened by repetition and practice. Repetition and practice are important when considering the learning curve (Fig. 2.1).

THE LEARNING CURVE

Consider an assembly plant making a certain component. This is the first time that the component has been made. The first component may take an hour before it is assembled satisfactorily. As the workers on the line become used to the tasks involved, the time to complete a unit will drop. The number of units completed per hour will rise until the maximum that even the most skilled worker can complete is reached. As time goes by, for any product or service the organization should be able to deliver it cheaper and better as employees learn and master the processes. Early prototypes will have bugs that need to be ironed out, and workers need training in order to produce at the most efficient rate.

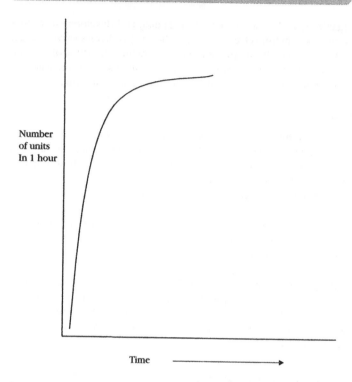

Fig. 2.1 The learning curve.

Irving[4] reports that the first fifty Boeing 747s to be built required a workforce of 27,500. By the time the breakeven four hundredth was produced the workforce was only 7500. That is the learning curve. As time goes by mistakes become less, and the time taken – especially in manufacturing – drops, thus aiding cash flows and recovery of costs.

In common with the term "training", learning is not confined to human beings – the vast majority of animal species learn at least part of their behavior. In Chapters 3 and 6 the idea will be put forward that it is not only the individuals within an organization who can learn, but also that the organization itself can learn.

The learning cycle and its application to training and development is discussed in Chapter 6.

Training

Training is very specific and is concerned with the mastering of a particular task or set of tasks.

At its most basic, training does not require understanding of the whys and wherefores. It is fairly easy to train a pigeon to select a particular shape from a collection of shapes or a Seeing Eye dog to guide a human being around obstacles or to sniff out drugs and explosives. The training process with animals involves rewards and punishments – a food treat as reward and a harsh word as a punishment. The pigeon and the dog can perform very competently, but there is no evidence to suggest that they know why they are behaving in this way, only that at some time in the past this type of behavior gained the animal a reward.

With humans, training that encompasses a degree of "why?" tends to be more effective than training that does not. However, one can train an individual to use a computer for word processing without that person understanding very much about how microprocessors actually work. Effective training provides the right degree of knowledge to underpin the task.

In the case of work-based training and development, punishment should never be used as this will cause the trainee to associate training with something unpleasant (punishment). Training and development may be challenging but it should never be unpleasant.

A distinction needs to be made between imposed punishments and rewards and the way an individual might "kick himself" when making a mistake or feel proud when all goes well.

It is possible to train an animal without consciously wanting to do so, often with negative results. More than one cat has learnt that the easiest way to have the door opened to go outside is to scratch the furniture. Cat scratches furniture – owner becomes annoyed – cat is put outside. It does not need this to happen many times before the cat will scratch the furniture in order to be put outside.

The effectiveness of training can be measured by examining what a person could do before the training and what he or she can do after it.

The difference may be in being actually able to perform a new task or an improvement in the manner of carrying out an old task.

Development

Development is a process in which learning occurs through experience and where the results of the learning enhance not only the task skills of the individual but also his or her attitudes. Whereas training does not necessarily encompass the "why", development most certainly does. Development provides the individual with skills and attributes that can be changed to fit new circumstances.

Whereas training can be measured objectively (before the training Mary could not do X, after the training she can do X), development is much more subjective. Development not only provides skills but also changes the way the individual thinks and reasons. Training is mechanical; development is humanistic.[5] Training may be accomplished in a relatively short time-frame; in contrast, development – linked as it is to intellectual growth – takes much longer.

Education

Used in its formal sense, education is the broadening of the knowledge and skills base of the individual (and indeed the group) with the objective of the individual functioning in and being a benefit to the society he or she lives in.

Development, as discussed earlier, is a process in which learning occurs through experience and where the results of the learning enhance not only the task skills of the individual but also his or her attitudes. Education is about individuals learning the norms operating in their society. Education is an investment by a society into its members with the ultimate aim of benefiting that society.

Formal education is usually provided by or in conjunction with those who are in charge of a particular society.

In organizational terms, much of development is akin to education in that it is concerned with attitudes, etc.

Coaching

Like training, coaching is concerned with skills, whether they are sporting skills or work skills. Every top-class athlete has a coach who works with him or her to improve technique. Coaching was an important part of apprenticeship schemes, as described in the next chapter. Coaching has seen a resurgence in recent years as organizations realize that it is an ideal method of transferring the skills and knowledge of older and more experienced employees to new hires. It also helps ensure that the intellectual capital of the organization is not diminished when an employee retires or leaves, as the skills and knowledge will have been passed on through the coaching process.

Mentoring

What coaching is to training, mentoring is to development. A mentor is not concerned solely with improving skills and performance in a narrow range of tasks but with the development of the whole individual. A mentor is an experienced person other than the individual's manager who provides counsel and guidance to assist the individual in his or her growth within the organization.

It is important that the mentor does not have a line management relationship with the individual, because that could cause a conflict of interest. Mentoring is covered in more detail in Chapter 6.

KEY LEARNING POINTS

» Training and development is the means by which an organization invests in its employees.

» In addition to the tangible assets such as buildings and cash, organizations also possess intangible assets such as "intellectual capital".

» The value of intangible assets may be far greater than that of tangible assets.

» Learning is the process by which behavior and attitudes are changed.

» As time goes by, for any product or service the organization should be able to deliver it cheaper and better as employees learn and master the processes.

» Training is very specific and is concerned with the mastering of a particular task or set of tasks.

- Development is a process in which learning occurs through experience and where the results of the learning enhance not only the task skills of the individual but also his or her attitudes.
- Training can be measured objectively whilst the measurement of development is much more subjective.
- Coaching is the process of transferring the skills and knowledge of older and more experienced employees to the less experienced through a close relationship – usually face-to-face.
- A mentor is an experienced person other than the individual's manager who provides counsel and guidance to assist the individual in his or her growth within the organization.

NOTES

1 Andrew Mayo (1998) *Creating a Training and Development Strategy*. Chartered Institute of Personnel and Development, London.
2 Clive Irving (1993) *Wide Body: The Making of the Boeing 747*. Hodder & Stoughton, London.
3 R. Thomson (1959) *The Psychology of Thinking*. Penguin, London.
4 Irving, *ibid.*
5 R. Lessem (1990) *Developmental Management*. Blackwell, Oxford.

The Evolution of Training and Development

The chapter considers how training and development has evolved. It explains:

» how the apprenticeship system was developed;
» the need for technical education and training brought about by the Industrial Revolution;
» the growth of universal education;
» the development of in-house training and continuous professional development; and
» the increasing use of computers and the Internet to support training and development.

BEHAVIOR AND SELF-ACTUALIZATION

In many respects the story of training and development is as old as the human race itself. Within the earliest human groupings there was a social structure that is not too different from what we know today. Mark Nicholson[1] of the London Business School writes that, although humans have evolved technologically, psychologically our species has not progressed very far from the tribalism of the Stone Age.

Within any primate grouping (and, biologically, humans are primates) one of the roles of adults is education of the young. One of the reasons why human children remain within the family grouping for as long as they do may be connected with the amount of learning that the youngsters need in order to function as members of society. Whilst much of social behavior appears innate there are also cultural norms and values that need to be imparted from generation to generation as a process of socialization.

One major difference between human behavior and that of other primates appears to be in the importance of *self-actualization*. Self-actualization is the final stage in the well-known "hierarchy of needs" developed by Abraham Maslow[2] in 1970. Unlike the lower-level needs of sustenance, safety, belonging, and esteem – all of which can be discerned to a greater or lesser degree in other primates such as gorillas and chimpanzees – self-actualization appears to be confined to humans. It is the need to fulfill one's potential, to push at the boundaries – it is a natural consequence of curiosity.

To be able to fulfill one's potential requires knowledge not only about oneself but also about where one fits within a social group. The acquisition of such knowledge comes about through education.

EARLY WORKPLACE TRAINING

Universal formal education is a fairly recent phenomenon in the West (but there are still many parts of the world where even a basic formal education is unavailable to most people). On the other hand, the importance and need for work-based training in order to pass on skills and knowledge has been recognized since the earliest times for which we have records.

Parents have always passed on skills to their children. One of the roles of a parent is to transmit to their offspring the basic social norms and the skills required for life. What developed as human social groupings became larger and more complex as the formalization of the means of acquiring the skills that society requires.

From the fourteenth century onwards in Europe, the apprenticeship system of learning the skills of a craft or trade from experts in the field by working with them for a set period of time became an important means by which skills were passed down. It was a system used extensively by the craft guilds in the Middle Ages. The word "guild" is derived from the German *Gilde* or *Hansa*, words referring to caravans of merchant traders. The Middle Ages saw the rise of craft guilds, which included in their membership all those engaged in any particular craft, and which monopolized the making and selling of a particular product within the cities in which they were organized.

The members of a craft guild were divided into three classes: masters, journeymen, and apprentices. The master owned the raw material and the tools, and sold the goods manufactured in his own shop for profit. The journeymen and apprentices lived in the master's house. The apprentices, who were beginners in the trade and learnt it under the direction of the master, usually received only their board in return for the work they did. In many cases the apprentice was indentured to the master, the apprentice's parents paying the master a sum of money. During the time span of the indenture the apprentice received no wages and was legally bound to the master who would train the apprentice in the particular trade. After an apprentice had completed his training he became a journeyman and was paid a fixed wage for his labor. In time a journeyman might become a master. However, it was to the advantage of those who were already masters not to increase their own number so that the conditions under which a journeyman might become a master were difficult. After the fourteenth century the requirements became so severe that it was virtually impossible for any journeyman to become a master. New masters tended to come from the master's own offspring.

THE INDUSTRIAL REVOLUTION

The Industrial Revolution during the nineteenth century was a time of considerable technological progress and migration of labor facilitated by the steamships and the railways – themselves products of the Industrial Revolution. The concept of a seven-year indenture became impossible to sustain, especially as changes in the legal status of individuals made binding a person to the same master difficult to enforce.

The new mechanical and engineering trades needed a means of training workers, especially those who migrated into them from agricultural work. A distinct differentiation between skilled and unskilled workers was a feature of the factories that sprang up throughout Europe and North America. The lowliest workers received just enough training to carry out their tasks, but there was a need for skilled engineers and designers. Apprenticeships were seen as a highly beneficial method of providing a skilled workforce in those trades that demanded skill and of retaining the knowledge and experience of older workers.

No longer was the apprentice tied to a master, although his (and very occasionally her) parents might have to pay a sum to the owner of the enterprise. The apprentice would be paired with an experienced worker who would train and teach him. Apprenticeships up until quite recently tended to be male dominated, but women entering factory work or domestic service would often be partnered with an older lady on a more informal basis.

THE GROWTH OF UNIVERSAL EDUCATION

One consequence of the Industrial Revolution and the advance of technology was the need for a better-educated general population. Even unskilled tasks began to need a rudimentary ability to read and write. Whereas policies of many governments up to the end of the eighteenth century had been antagonistic to the idea of universal education – on the grounds that increased knowledge might ferment revolution – by the beginning of the nineteenth century it was beginning to be realized that the more educated the population, the better the economy.

The first nation to begin to move to universal educational provision was Prussia. The Prussian Law of 1810 was a reaction against the country's military defeat by France, led by Napoleon, and provided for state secondary (high) schools in addition to primary (elementary) education. Other countries also set up state primary schools or gave public financial aid to church schools in the early nineteenth century, including Denmark in 1807 as well as France and Great Britain in the 1830s.

Universal elementary education required a degree of compulsion, especially as young people were able to begin their working careers much earlier than they can today, at least in the developed world. To commence work at the age of 12 was not uncommon. For many poorer families educating a child meant the loss of a potential earner in the household. Laws that made school attendance compulsory were passed in Massachusetts in 1851, to be followed by other American states between 1864 and 1890 (with the exception of the southern states, which delayed compulsion until the early twentieth century). In Europe, compulsion was applied in 1868 in Prussia, in England and Wales in the 1870s (Scotland and Northern Ireland had and retain their own unique system of education), and in France and other countries in the 1880s.

Secondary schools had been state institutions in France as in Prussia from the early nineteenth century, although they were fee-paying. In England they remained private institutions until much later. Opportunities for free secondary education for some talented children from state primary schools were provided from the late nineteenth century, but universal secondary education did not become general in most European countries until after 1945.

It is salutary to contemplate that this was only so recent. The exponential increase in technology since 1945 could not have occurred without a comprehensive system of universal education. In the much more egalitarian social conditions of the late twentieth century, knowledge and expertise could not be confined to a select few.

THE NEED FOR WORK-BASED TRAINING AND DEVELOPMENT

The formal education system in nearly every part of the world is aimed at the younger members of society. The education system is designed to provide the basic skills of mathematics, reading, science, and the arts. What the system cannot provide is the specific skills required for particular jobs. Provision in this area is best accomplished through specific programs geared to the job and the employer.

This does not mean that there is no link between formal education and training and development. The better formal education a person has received, the more honed will be his or her basic skills and the ability to reason and analyze. A person with a good basic education is likely to be more accomplished at learning new skills than somebody who lacks the basics.

The remainder of this book is concerned with training and development that is work-related, but the importance of a good grounding in basic skills should never be underemphasized. The great leader Winston Spencer Churchill (who did not shine at school according to his reminiscences in his book *My Early Life*) stressed the importance of being competent at using one's native language in both written and verbal form. He went as far as to hint, hopefully jokingly, that a failure to speak and write competently should lead to punishment for the offending child. The events of World War II and the increasing technological aspect to industry that the war demonstrated showed that a more educated population was no longer a luxury but a necessity. Social pressures and changes throughout the world also demanded that all citizens be granted access to universal education, regardless of age, gender, or social position.

VOCATIONAL TRAINING

What a formal education system could not accomplish was the training of engineers, mechanics, and draftsmen (still male-oriented professions in the nineteenth and twentieth centuries). Even if the resources had been available, the pace of change was so rapid that the formal education system could not keep up.

Employers who needed the skills but lacked the resources to provide the necessary training in all but the most work-related tasks, and who were reluctant to allow staff time off for training, were nevertheless prepared to help fund the development of vocational training institutes – often called Mechanics' Institutes. Employees who wished to further their careers were encouraged to attend such institutes in their own time, usually in the evening. From the 1880s onwards such vocational institutes were established in towns and cities the length and breadth of North America and Europe.

An example is the Canadian town Sault Ste Marie, where a branch of the Mechanics' Institute was formed in 1890 linked to the local library. It is recorded that Francis H. Clergue, a local industrialist, received the thanks of the Mechanics' Institute in 1895 when he obtained 15 subscriptions and by 1896 owned a collection of 967 books.

Records of the Crystal Palace in London, the site of the Great Exhibition, state that on 10 June 1863 the place was visited by more than 1000 members of the Society of Arts and representatives of the Literary, Scientific, and Mechanics' Institutes as well as various mayors and others.

In the USA the development of vocational training to meet the needs of industry received considerable political backing. Massachusetts's Governor Douglas appointed a commission in 1905 to study the need for vocational education. The commission was led by C.A. Prosser (the initiator of the American Vocational Association). The commission set up several public hearings in the state – which indicated widespread interest in vocational education, lack of skilled workers in industries, and the fact that public schools were doing little to meet the needs of industry and society at the time. The work of this group led the way for other states to form similar groups to study vocational education.

In 1914, President Woodrow Wilson set up the Commission on National Aid to Vocational Education to study the need for different types of vocational education and the conditions under which federal funding should be granted. The efforts of this group influenced the passage of the Smith-Hughes Act that was instrumental in developing vocational education in the USA. The Act allocated $7.2mn per year of matching funds to states for agriculture, home economics, and trade and industrial education. As a result of this Act a Federal Board for Vocational Education was established. The Act required that states submit a state plan for funding annually. The funding was for education of less than college grade and designed to meet the needs of persons over 14 years of age (far younger than today) who had entered or who were preparing to enter the workforce.

UNIVERSITIES AND COLLEGES

The first universities as we know them today were established in Europe during the Middle Ages to educate the sons of the nobility and wealthy merchants (daughters did not receive this type of education until the late nineteenth and early twentieth centuries). The education was classical in nature, being based on philosophy and literature. Such a system was ill-equipped to cope with the technological demands of the Industrial Revolution and the organizations that were formed to manufacture and trade on a scale far greater than had been experienced in the past.

Whilst Mechanics' Institutes could provide a rudimentary technical training, they could not provide the broad scientific and technical foundations that were beginning to be needed for a wider range of occupations. Various types of technical colleges and institutes were developed in both North America and Europe to provide further and higher education that concentrated on the practical applications of science and technology. MIT and Caltech in the USA, and UMIST in England, are amongst the best known in the world.

MIT (Massachusetts Institute of Technology), an establishment with a global reputation, was founded in 1861. UMIST (University of Manchester Institute of Science & Technology) was founded in 1824 as the Manchester Mechanics' Institution. In the early years of the twentieth century it established a reputation as one of the major centers for technical education in the UK and the rest of Europe. In 1956 it became the Manchester College of Science & Technology, and in 1966 it became a part of the University of Manchester and took its present title.

Caltech was founded by Amos Troop in 1891 and given the name of Troop University. In 1907 the astronomer Ellery Hale, the first director of the Mount Wilson Observatory, became a member of Troop's board of trustees and envisioned molding it into a first-class institution for engineering and scientific research and education. By 1921, Hale had been joined by chemist Arthur A. Noyes and physicist Robert A. Millikan. These three men set the university, which by then had been renamed the California Institute of Technology (CIT), on the course to international recognition.

Unlike many of the universities, these institutions sought links with commercial organizations. By the 1950s the UK – which had led the Industrial Revolution – had developed a system of further-education colleges of technology, polytechnics, and universities in a rather hierarchical configuration. The most able went to the universities, whilst further education was for those who had left school without the necessary qualifications for polytechnic or university entry. If so motivated these individuals could gain further qualifications through full- or part-time study, often financed through the public purse.

The colleges of further education and the polytechnics sought ever-closer links with industry and commerce, links that traditional universities were slower to make. These links were strengthened by the introduction of degree "sandwich" courses – whereby the student spent part of the course in full-time study and the remainder on a work placement.

The vast majority of the UK polytechnics became universities in the 1990s but retained their links with the world of business and commerce – links that the more traditional universities have now made. Complaints and comments about "ivory towers" are now far fewer as higher education has seen the benefits of working with industry and commerce. These benefits are not just financial through sponsorship and professorial chairs but also in staff exchanges and research partnerships.

In 1969, in an effort to assist those who had not received the opportunity for higher education, the UK government founded the Open University (OU) using television and radio in addition to printed material as the medium for study. Since then the OU has provided higher education opportunities for two million students ranging in age from 17 to 94, as well as serving as a model for similar enterprises overseas.

IN-HOUSE PROGRAMS

The alternative to having employees taking time off work for training and study, or having to use their leisure time, is for the organization to facilitate the training itself. The latter years of the twentieth century saw a huge proliferation in both organization-based programs and companies offering training and development outside the formal education system that offered to design and implement such training courses for organizations. By providing in-house provision resourced either internally or externally, the organization can ensure that training meets the needs of the organization. As systems and procedures change, training needs are identified and met in a manner that is contextualized to the particular organization.

CONTINUOUS PROFESSIONAL DEVELOPMENT (CPD)

In a large number of careers and professions, the information and skills learnt upon entry rapidly become out of date. As the pace of technological change has increased so the lifespan of a particular piece of knowledge has lessened. This has generated a need for continuous professional development, a process that recognizes that there are lifelong learning and training needs.

Many professions and employers now require members and employees to undertake regular CPD to ensure that their knowledge and skills are as up to date as possible. CPD is one of the most important developments in training and development today, together with a growing appreciation that the learning methodologies used in schools, colleges, and universities are far from ideal when dealing with employees who have a wealth of experience. From the 1970s onwards it began to become apparent that adults learn in very different ways to children and that work-based training and development could not use the same techniques as schools.

The linking of CPD, work-based training, and learning styles forms the basis for Chapter 6.

THE INTERNET AND E-LEARNING

It may well be that you are reading this as part of an e-book. The ability of information and communication technology to support training and development is being exploited more and more.

From the 1990s, the practicality of online delivery and support for training and development programs has been increasing rapidly, and the e-dimension of training and development forms the subject of Chapter 4.

TRAINING AND DEVELOPMENT TIME LINE

- » *ca.* **1400**: Development of guilds and apprenticeships; foundation of early universities in Europe
- » *ca.* **1820**: Industrial Revolution
- » **1824**: Manchester Mechanics' Institute founded; later became Manchester College of Science & Technology
- » **1861**: Massachusetts Institute of Technology (MIT) founded
- » *ca.* **1870**: Beginnings of compulsory primary (elementary) education
- » **1891**: Troop University founded
- » **1907**: Hale joins Troop University and it becomes Caltech (CIT)
- » **1914**: President Woodrow Wilson set up the Commission on National Aid to Vocational Education
- » **1939–45**: World War II
- » **1966**: Manchester College of Science & Technology becomes UMIST
- » **1969**: UK establishes the Open University
- » **1970s**: Studies into how adults learn
- » **1980s**: Growth in continuous professional development (CPD) mirrors rapid growth in technology
- » **1990s**: UK polytechnics become universities; e-learning systems are developed

KEY LEARNING POINTS

- » Education has gone from being the preserve of a small elite to a right for the whole population.
- » There has been a steady growth in vocational education as the technological needs of commerce have increased.
- » Adult learners need techniques different from those used to teach children.
- » Continuous professional development (CPD) is now a requirement for many jobs and professions.

» There has been growth in the use of the Internet to support training and development programs.

NOTES

1 Mark Nicholson (2000) *Managing the Human Animal*. Crown, NewYork.
2 Abraham Maslow (1970) *Motivation and Personality*. Harper & Row, NewYork.

The E-Dimension of Training and Development

The chapter considers how the e-dimension to training and development has evolved. It explains how:

» computers and the Internet have led to a requirement for training in the skills needed to use them effectively;
» the use of computers and the Internet has provided new methods for delivering training on a variety of subjects;
» the use of simulations and the ability of trainees to work at their own pace is cost-effective; and
» the use of computer-based training programs can lead to problems of isolation that can impact on the individual trainee's motivation.

THE CHALLENGE OF THE INTERNET

The rapid growth of information and communication technology (ICT) from the 1980s has had two major implications for training and development.

Training for the users of ICT

In the early 1980s few people had used a computer. Typewriters, telex machines, early photocopiers, and telephones constituted the main form of office technology. By the year 2000 there can have been few people across the globe who had not at least had contact with a computer. In the developed world, not only had nearly every office access to a personal computer but also so had a great many homes. The number of people who were online to the Internet was growing almost exponentially. As David Stauffer[1] has reported in his study of the Internet service provider (ISP) AOL, that company had over 20 million subscribers by 2000. Such rates of growth are unprecedented.

The Internet, which only really entered the public arena in the early 1990s, is now an everyday tool for business, pleasure, and academia. The fact that the ExpressExec series is not just printed material but available in electronic formats – an idea hardly contemplated in 1990 – is testament to the ways in which the Internet and its associated services have been harnessed. The synergy between computer, television, and telephone technologies has seen the way people communicate change almost beyond recognition.

To take one example, in 2002 the postal delivery part of the Royal Mail in the UK stated that one of the main reasons for the huge losses it was making was the increase in the number of e-mails being sent, with a commensurate drop in the number of actual letters.

Such technological growth has led to the need to retrain and reskill large numbers of employees into new skills related to ICT. Developments have also altered school curricula, as computer skills are nowadays a very important requirement for those entering work. Fortunately children appear to be able to pick up the necessary computer and associated technology skills very easily – so much so that if you want to have a video cassette recorder programmed it appears that the average 8-year-old is often far more competent than his or her parents.

There has been a huge market in the provision of computer and Internet courses and programs of study. Nearly every college and adult education institution in the world has offered a package aimed at bringing people up to speed with the new technologies. The release of new versions of software such as Windows® or Microsoft Office® is followed by the provision of updating courses for users of the previous editions.

The Internet as a training and development delivery tool

The second major implication of the growth in Internet use is the way it has facilitated changes in the methods by which training and development are actually delivered.

The 1960s saw the introduction of rudimentary teaching machines based not on computer technology but using microfiche technology – in effect to make semi-interactive books. The machines were of little practical use and never gained any prominence. Of more practical use were improvements in language teaching using tape-recorder technology as part of language laboratories. Whilst crude by today's standards, these early language labs showed that technology had a role to play in the actual teaching process.

Two types of training make extensive use of computers and the Internet. CBT (computer-based training) and CAL (computer-assisted learning) are similar terms for the use of computers to assist in the learning process. If there is a difference between them it is relative – CBT may have much more of the complete training page computer-based than CAL; and CBT is often focused on tasks whereas CAL may have a broader focus and be more developmental, as described in Chapter 2.

THE RISE OF COMPUTERS

Trainers began to discover that the computer could be an immense aid to the learning process for a number of reasons, as outlined below.

Computer simulations

There are many tasks that are much better learnt on a simulator. Pilots changing from one aircraft type to another carry out the majority of their training on a simulator. Whilst the costs of such simulators are huge, the cost of a mistake on a real aircraft would be much greater.

The ability of computer simulation to answer "what if?" questions without risk is one of the major benefits in the training process. All manner of situations can be simulated, from changing procedures to complex financial modeling. Time can be contracted so that a whole production cycle, for example, can be compressed into a short time period on the computer. Many management games that model company behavior over time make full use of the computer's ability to compress time.

It must be remembered, however, that the output from a computer is only as good as the quality of its programming.

Instant feedback on responses

The sooner a person receives feedback on his or her performance at a new task, the easier it is for that person to modify behavior in order to improve. The immediacy of a response from the computer can thus aid the learning process.

There is a downside, however. The computer can often indicate whether a response is correct or not and the possible implications of doing something wrong. It cannot enter into a discussion about what has happened, and why. That is an important part of learning – hence the need for human contact in the training process. The technology can assist the trainer but can rarely replace the need for an explanation from another human being.

Less face-to-face contact with trainees

Trainers and trainees can be linked using e-mail or through video-conferencing. For example, the Millennium Institute at the University of the Highlands & Islands (UHI) in Scotland makes extensive use of video-conferenced lectures and tutorials to bring university-level education to those in the more remote areas of the country. There is no longer the need to use a studio for tutorials – the tutor and student need only have webcams on their monitors in the home or in the office. A fundamental aim of UHI is to widen access to lifelong learning for the people of the Highlands and Islands, and modern technology is making that aim easier to realize.

The Internet as a research tool

The vast amount of information on the Internet means that a trainee anywhere in the world has access to a huge virtual library if he or she has the necessary skills to conduct searches. Whilst contemporary search engines have made the job of finding the right information easier, there is still a need for initial training on the best techniques for finding precisely what is desired.

Individual progress rates

In a conventional classroom, the speed of learning tends to be that of the slowest trainee. The Internet can free the trainer to spend time with those who need it whilst others progress at their own faster rate. This means that the frustration of all parties in the traditional scenario – the fast because they are held back, the slow because the lesson progresses too quickly, and the trainer who feels that he or she is not able to meet the needs of every class member – is alleviated. The pressure on a trainee in this type of training is internal and people respond to internal pressures much better than they do when pressurized from outside.

IMPLICATIONS FOR LEARNER MOTIVATION

Jim Stewart and Rosemary Winter,[2] amongst others, point out that maintaining the motivation of the learner/trainee is of vital importance and is especially problematic in training programs where there is little or no face-to-face contact. Whilst computer-based training is highly cost-effective and allows the trainee to progress at his or her own pace, it can be a lonely experience.

As a major supplier of "distance learning" in the UK, the Open University (OU) recognized this problem right from its inception. In addition to providing formal tutorials held in local centers (usually at weekends or in the evening so as not to encroach on work commitments), it encourages students to form self-help groups – in order to assist motivation as much as to discuss program content issues.

Maintaining motivation through computer-based training programs is a matter of striking a balance between the advantages of open/distance learning and the benefits of meeting with one's peers. It may well be that physical meetings are impossible to arrange, especially if the trainees are widely scattered. The imaginative use of newsgroups, dedicated chat rooms, and webcams can help alleviate the possible isolation that an individual trainee can experience.

Efficient as computers are, they cannot provide reassurance to a trainee with a problem or who feels that progress is not being made. Despite the wonders of technology there is likely to remain an important human element in the provision of effective training.

HOME WORKING AND TRAINING

Information and communication technology has allowed access to the employment market for those who previously had difficulty working at conventional jobs. People having to care for young children or sick or elderly relatives, the disabled, and those living in remote areas can find opportunities, especially for part-time work, by adding a PC, a modem, a facsimile machine, and perhaps a PC-top camera to their home office. One estimate puts the number of people working from home in the US and UK populations at 7%.

There are many tasks, especially within the service sector, that do not require attendance at a physical office in the conventional sense. The same technology that allows the person to gain employment is well placed to provide the necessary training and continuous professional development (CPD) opportunities

The problems of trainee *motivation* apply also to home workers who may have little or no face-to-face contact with colleagues and must rely mainly on e-mail. In some parts of northern Scotland, for example, the concept of a *telecottage* has been pioneered. In a telecottage, a group of those who would normally work at home for different organizations meet to carry out their tasks in a central point locally. The telecottage can be fitted out with the latest in ICT and the purchase of equipment can benefit from sharing and economies of scale. Such developments also often attract government funding as they serve to improve the local economy by providing much-needed jobs. Telecottages also provide an excellent base for group-based training using computers and the Internet as a means of delivery. This is another area in which the Millennium Institute of the UHI has played a leading role – a number of such centers have been established throughout the Highlands and Islands region.

BEST PRACTICE CASE
TCM.com Inc. (Canada)

There are many excellent organizations offering computer-based training and computer-assisted learning. TCM.com Inc. of Canada is one such provider of high-quality training, offering e-learning courses in a variety of computer-related topics, including:

- end-user business skills development;
- end-user desktop computing;
- end-user home and small business operations;
- insurance professional development; and
- technical development (general and for the Web).

These are all delivered in an Internet-based format. The courses are self-paced so that the pressure on the trainee to perform is internal rather than external (see earlier).

Before taking a course the potential trainee undertakes an *assessment task*. The results of the test reveal to the trainee what parts of the course he or she needs to take. A post-test is also available so that the trainee can see how well the material has been mastered.

- *Exercises*. The course itself contains exercises based on the particular application page for which training is required.
- *Questions*. True/false, matching, and fill-in-the-blank questions are liberally included throughout the courses, enabling the trainee to engage in the learning process and to measure personal progress.
- *Simulations*. The courses contain a series of task-based simulations to allow the trainee to work with "what if?" situations as mentioned earlier in this chapter. This allows the trainee to gain as near a real-life experience as possible without the danger of permanently ruining an employer's documents or processes.
- *Bookmarking*. The client technology recognizes the point the trainee has reached in a course and tracks his or her progress.

The next time the trainee accesses the course there is no need to remember the exact point at which the previous session finished.

» *Search*. The trainee can research a topic of interest in any or all of the courses, enabling the easy retrieval of information.

The benefits that TCM claim for the approach are:

» **Accessibility**. Vision-impaired trainees can use a text-reader program to read the text-only version of a course. This enables trainees to access the various course features by using command keys to navigate, search the glossary, and answer course questions.

» **Use of time and controlling the pace**. The trainee can access the course at any time of the day or night, and work at a personal pace. The trainee is in control of his or her time.

» **Cost-effectiveness**. The system is geared for both individual and corporate use. The ability to work at the trainee's own pace and at the times he or she (and the employer if necessary) chooses makes this a very cost-effective method of training. The use of questions to provide feedback ensures that the trainee makes progress with the most efficient use of time.

» **Focus on what the trainee needs**. As the trainee is in control of progress, it is possible to focus on individual needs rather than those of other class members as in a more traditional training system. Not every trainee will have a need to access the same material at the same time. Using the Internet as a research tool means that all members of a training cohort can access what they need and when they need it.

» **Continuing education**. This type of training forms a useful part of continuous professional development as discussed in Chapter 3.

TCM understands the problems of obtaining access to high-quality training at low cost. Modern work patters often necessitate access to quality training at any time, anywhere, at reasonable cost, and to be able to undertake courses at home or at the workplace.

TCM also offers the ECDL (European Computer Driving License) – often referred to as the International Computer Driving License outside of Europe. The ECDL forms a best practice case study in Chapter 6.

KEY LEARNING POINTS

» The increasing use of computers and the Internet has led to a requirement for training in the ways the technology is used in business.

» The new technologies have also changed the manner in which training can be delivered.

» ICT can benefit trainees by:
- allowing them to work at their own pace;
- providing the opportunity for simulation;
- allowing the trainee to choose the time and place for the training; and
- providing a research facility through the Internet.

» Computers and the Internet can aid but are unlikely to remove the human element, which is so vital for motivation from training programs.

NOTES

1 David Stauffer (2000) *Business the AOL Way*. Capstone, Oxford.

2 Jim Stewart and Rosemary Winter (1995) 'Open and distance learning'. In Truelove, S. (ed.) *Handbook of Training Development*, 2nd edn. Blackwell, Oxford.

The Global Dimension of Training and Development

The chapter considers the global dimension to training and development. It explains how:

» organizations need to take cultural differences into account when delivering training and development to staff from other countries;
» to minimize the use of idioms when delivering to staff from other countries; and
» British Airways developed a robust training and development program for supervisors and managers from across the airline's global network.

INTRODUCTION

The ExpressExec title *Going Global* (2002) defines globalization as the process whereby organizations offer their products and services on a global rather than a local basis. As this process continues, organizations are having to consider the international dimension to their training and development plans.

Organizations that commence operations in countries other than their home country have to take into account the differences in customs, legislation, customer behavior, and employment practices. There is also a need to ensure that the foreign employees understand the policies and procedures of the organization. One of the major issues for any organization that commences global operations is the need to adapt to a new culture.

CULTURE

Culture can be defined as the "way we do things around here" and differs from place to place across the globe, between ethnic groups and between organizations. There is, fortunately, a wealth of material on managing cultural differences and the reader is advised to consult the ExpressExec title *Managing Diversity* (Chapters 5 and 6), as well as *Riding the Waves of Culture* by Fons Trompenaars, *When Cultures Collide* by Richard D. Lewis, and *Managing Cultural Differences* by Philip Harris and Robert Morgan (details of these texts are given in Chapter 9).

It would be a foolish organization that did not take account of the culture in which it was planning to operate. Different cultures have different attitudes to training, development, and education.

Cultural issues
Hierarchy

In a particular culture it may be necessary to train a person higher up in the hierarchy before somebody lower down, not because that person needs the training or development first but because of his or her position.

Attitudes to gender

Training and development should be provided in line with strict equal opportunities policies. In cases where the culture does not usually provide equal opportunities, the organization should be sensitive in the way it explains why it intends to insist on equal opportunities being applied to all aspects of its operation and not just training and development. Good training and development can be very productive in helping to change attitudes and in providing opportunities for development to those who might be denied such opportunities were it not for the fact that they are employed by the organization.

Attitudes to age and experience

There may well be issues not only of the order in which employees are offered training and development opportunities but also the age and experience of the deliverers of such programs. This can be a considerable issue in development programs where the focus is wider than just training for a particular task. Many US and European organizations provide management development programs to junior staff who show management potential. There are areas of the world where this would normally be unacceptable given the way hierarchies are arranged in those areas. Sensitivity is required especially in convincing senior staff that providing development opportunities to their juniors should not be considered a threat to the senior person's position.

Attitudes to the education process

If employees have been used to an education process that is formal and based on examinations/tests, they might not consider more informal training and development programs to carry much credibility. The training methods used may need to be adapted at first to correspond to what the trainees are used to.

The language of delivery

Organizations need to consider the language that is used in program delivery and for the supporting materials. Ideally these should be in the trainee's native language. It may well be, however, that if the trainees have proficiency in the native language of the organization then the delivery and the materials will be in that language.

It needs to be borne in mind that most people who learn a foreign language may have proficiency in its formal aspects but not be proficient with its idioms. We tend to speak idiomatically even when we write formally. Those delivering training need to avoid the use of idioms as much as possible. Even throughout the English-speaking world there are considerable linguistic differences. The concept that the USA and the UK are "divided by a common language" is very apt. (Christopher Davies[1] has produced a humorous but useful guide to how the British can avoid making mistakes in the USA, and vice versa; it is a good text for those who live on one English-speaking side of the Atlantic and are working or vacationing on the other side.)

Culture and HRM

It is not difficult to discover the cultural norms of an area and it is nearly always worth taking the time to do so. Training and development that can be related to the culture of an area is always going to have a better chance of succeeding than trying to use the programs and language from one area in another without modification. Pat Joynt and Bob Morton[2] have edited a useful volume, *The Global HR Manager*, that considers the issues facing those responsible for HRM (human resource management)/personnel function in organizations operating on a global stage. They have introduced what they call "the seven Cs" of international HRM:

» competition
» culture
» communications
» competencies – implications for training and development
» compensation
» careers – implications for training and development
» collaboration.

Of these, "competencies" and "careers" have direct implications for training and development. Competence is an area considered in Chapter 6. The link between training and development and careers is a close one, especially when continuous professional development (CPD) is taken into account.

DEVELOPMENT OF A GLOBAL TRAINING PROGRAM AT BRITISH AIRWAYS

Best practice case

Background information

British Airways (BA) was created as a nationalized airline by the merger of British European Airways (BEA) and the British Overseas Airways Corporation (BOAC) in 1974 as part of a government rationalization of the UK air transportation industry. As a nationalized airline, British Airways had a reputation for poor service and inflexible attitudes, but the privatization of the airline by the Conservative government in February 1987 was to change the image of the company.

The sale of shares in the airline raised over £900 million for the government. Many of the shares were sold to members of the public as part of Prime Minister Margaret Thatcher's concept of a share-owning democracy. British Airways had been preparing for the privatization for some time and was determined to become a customer-centered player in the global airline market.

The antecedents of British Airways provided the airline with an extensive route network especially in areas where the UK had possessed colonial interests. In a surprise move, within a few months of the privatization the company acquired the major UK independent international carrier British Caledonian, thus gaining extra routes and further capacity at London's rapidly growing second airport, London Gatwick.

The transformation from a nationalized state air carrier to become a benchmark for innovation and service was rapid. British Airways embarked on a policy of growth by partnerships and franchises both in the UK and abroad. As examples, by 1993 it held a 31% stake in Air Russia, a subsidiary named British Asia Airways, a considerable stake in Brymon European (a UK-based regional operator), a 49% stake in Deutsche BA in Germany, plus links with a number of other European and US carriers. These partnerships and alliances have been a major trend in the airline industry in recent years.

Staff diversity

In order to provide a first-class service, British Airways has had to manage a diverse staff base across the world. It employs a considerable number of locally based staff both on the ground and as cabin crew/flight attendants usually flying to and from their own country. One of the features of the franchise system has been that the aircraft of the franchisee fly in British Airways livery and the staff dress in BA uniforms, so it is important from a customer-care standpoint that the service received is identical to the standard BA product. As that service has been rightly considered amongst the best in the world, the franchisee staff must meet the high standards demanded of British Airways' own staff.

Continuous professional development: FOS program

One of the prerequisites of maintaining high standards, according to the US management guru Tom Peters, is an emphasis on initial training and continuous professional development (CPD) – the importance of CPD having been stressed in earlier chapters of this book. Following the Gulf War crisis of the early 1990s, British Airways (which had been running an entry-level management/supervisory program entitled FOS – *Fundamentals of Supervision*) decided to re-tender for the program and chose a consortium from Oxford in the UK to design and develop, in close consultation with the BA training staff in London, a re-launch of the program suitable for staff from any part of the network.

The new FOS program was designed around modules covering:

» the context of management;
» managing people;
» finance and law;
» marketing; and
» the management of information.

Each module was assessed through a formative assignment, whose mark did not count towards the final grade, and an end-of-module assignment, the mark for which was used to determine the final result. The final qualification was a Certificate in Management Studies (CMS), awarded at first by one of the UK awarding bodies and later on by one of the UK universities.

Each module also included a half-day workshop. Initially workshops were held in London, Newcastle, Manchester (all in the UK), and Berlin for a German cohort. All participants were divided into cohorts of about twelve, each cohort having a dedicated academic tutor who delivered the seminars and marked the assignments.

Whilst the consortium put forward the names of suitable tutors, it was British Airways who interviewed them and made the final decision as to their suitability.

An important feature of the program was that it had to be accessible and relevant to any members of staff recommended by their line managers as being suitable for the level of training, no matter what their department or their place and country of work. Over the 1990s, participants included pilots, cabin crew/flight attendants, engineers, check-in staff, administrative staff, medical staff, sales representatives, and baggage personnel. The geographic range was huge, from Los Angeles to Tokyo and Berlin to Sydney, Australia, with every continent except Antarctica being represented. This meant that materials had to be prepared with very great care as motivational techniques and employment law often differ widely between regions. Assignments also needed to be assessed with cultural sensitivity. Much of the seminar time was taken up with exploring the balance between the cultural requirements of the particular region and the need to meet the BA culture, especially in respect of standards of customer care.

In addition to the workshop seminars, all participants attended a weekend (Friday through Sunday) residential period held in the Peak District of northern England. One of the objectives of the residential period was to introduce the participants to the team role and team-building techniques. Working in multidisciplinary and multicultural teams, the participants undertook both indoor exercises and discussions, and a day out on the Derbyshire moors where each team had to complete a series of tasks that involved map reading, rock climbing, caving, and abseiling. All these activities were arranged and supervised by qualified outdoor activity instructors and the program suffered no serious accidents.

The residential period, attended by three cohorts and their tutors at a time, also served to bring people from diverse and distant parts of the airline together. One of the major benefits reported by participants was the understanding that developed about other people's jobs and even their culture. In effect there was an extra training outcome from the program as the participants gained an understanding not just of other cultures but also other areas within the airline.

The whole thrust of the FOS program was that the skills and knowledge acquired should be applicable in the participant's work situation regardless of their department or geographic location. FOS was just one of the British Airways training initiatives of the 1990s that had staff flying into London for training; "Winning for Customers" was another program that was highly successful and actually involved not only all BA staff members but the staff of franchisees and major suppliers to the airline.

Such programs are very expensive, especially with up to 200 participants per year; but there is no doubt that the training costs were repaid by the standard of service for which British Airways became a watchword. Indeed, at a time when other airlines were losing money on a regular basis, British Airways was consistently profitable – showing how much of an investment carefully planned and implemented training can be.

Offered as it was to all suitable staff, FOS soon became very popular. Staff acquired management skills and the confidence to use them, and this transferred into the workplace. There was soon a waiting list for the program, especially from overseas staff.

Expansion of the program

In 1993 it was decided to expand the Berlin operation to include the United States, with a cohort operating out of the company's US headquarters in Queens, New York. The first cohort included staff from New York itself, Los Angeles, Miami, Atlanta, Washington DC, Seattle, and Toronto (Canada). By flying the tutor out to New York, money and perhaps more importantly staff time was saved and the seminars could be focused more directly on US issues. In time this operation was further expanded to include not just the United States (where it later operated out of Miami in order to assist flying in staff from the Caribbean and South/Central America) but also India, South Africa, and Australia.

The tutors involved in these overseas groups needed to adapt their methods of delivery to suit the region they were working in rather than using standard UK techniques. Whilst this was certainly a challenge it was one that they rose to. The writer has no doubt that the increasing demand for places on the program from overseas staff was in no small measure due to the fact that delivery was adapted to meet the cultural needs of the particular group.

The only FOS requirement for the members of these cohorts to visit the UK was for the residential weekend.

Re-evaluation of the program

In 1995 the program underwent a full evaluation. The materials that were in use were based on generic UK training packs. With a requirement to meet the needs of an increasing number of overseas participants, it was decided to rewrite the materials from scratch so as:

» to integrate them with the set of supervisory/management competencies that British Airways had been developing; and

» to be more explicit in the way overseas issues were covered and to further ensure that local issues were addressed where these differed from standard BA practice.

Final comments

The FOS program is a good example of how a training and development program can be developed for an international audience. The message was the same to all staff as it reflected the core values of the airline, and those remained the same wherever the company operated, but the manner in which it was put over could be such as to meet local needs. This required considerable study by the tutors and a very close liaison between them, the consortium administrators, and BA's own training department as the sponsors of the program.

One extremely important touch was the inclusion of a graduation ceremony where BA arranged for the attendance airfares and accommodation of all graduating participants (the success rate was well over 90%) and their partners plus the tutors and administrators. Certificates were presented by a senior manager, usually the CEO, thus underlining the importance the airline gave to the program. Nobody who wanted to undertake FOS and who was recommended by his or her manger was refused a place, at least on the waiting list. Despite the inclusion of a residential period that could be somewhat physical, culture, gender, and disabilities were all dealt with in a manner so that all participants, and of course British Airways, gained the maximum out of the program.

Whilst British Airways suffered a downturn in business after the tragedies of the terrorist attacks of 11 September 2001, the fact that so much time and effort has been devoted to training and developing staff gives the airline a considerable intangible asset in its human capital (see Chapter 2) that should assist business recovery.

BRITISH AIRWAYS TIME LINE

- **1991**: End of Gulf War (Desert Storm)
- **1992**: Re-tendering for entry-level management program (FOS); contract awarded to Oxford Consortium; cohorts in UK and Germany
- **1993**: First US cohort (New York)
- **1994**: Cohorts in UK, US (New York), and India (Delhi)
- **1995**: Australian cohort (Sydney) added; rewrite of program to fit in with new BA corporate objectives
- **1996**: US cohort moves from New York to Miami
- **1997**: South African cohort (Johannesburg) added

KEY LEARNING POINTS

- The FOS program at British Airways was a partnership between British Airways' own training staff and an outside training provider (the consortium).
- The program was designed to fit in with the values and aspirations of the airline.
- The issues of job and cultural diversity were allowed for at the very beginning of the program.
- The program was designed so that it could be delivered to discrete overseas cohorts in their own regions.

> » The tutors on the program needed to acquaint themselves with both the culture and operations of the company and those of the staff.
> » The program was open to all staff. The only requirement was motivation and a recommendation from the applicant's line manager.
> » The program not only developed skills, by bringing staff together it promoted an understanding of the role and culture of others.

NOTES

1 Christopher Davies (1997) *Divided by a Common Language*. Mayflower Press, Sarasota, FL.
2 Pat Joynt and Bob Morton (eds) (1999) *The Global HR Manager*. Chartered Institute of Personnel & Development, London.

The State of the Art

The chapter examines current thinking on training and development, including:

» the need to link training and development to organizational objectives;
» not using training and development as a reward or punishment;
» training needs analysis (TNA);
» the skills gap;
» the training cycle;
» learning styles;
» setting training objectives;
» evaluating training and development;
» experiential learning;
» action learning;
» competence approaches;
» development;
» mentors and mentoring; and
» the learning organization.

LINKS WITH OBJECTIVES

Companies wishing to undertake effective training and development need to plan the appropriate activities carefully to ensure maximum benefit.

No matter what the training and development activities are to be, they need to be devised in conjunction with overall aims and objectives of the organization. Strange as it might seem, there have been times when staff have been financed to undertake development activities that have no relation whatsoever to organizational objectives. It is permissible (as the Rover company did in the 1990s in the UK) to assist staff with learning opportunities of the staff's own choice when the staff were undertaking them in their own time. People who are interested in learning, even if it learning about a non-work related area, tend to be more motivated and better informed. However, when the organization is providing both time and finance then there should be a clear link between the training/development and the organization's objectives.

Training should be neither a punishment nor a reward. Training is provided to meet an organizational need. If an employee has made a mistake caused by a lack of skills or knowledge, then the question of why the person was undertaking a task for which he or she lacked the necessary skills should be asked of the line manger. Training should be provided but not as a punishment. Linking training to blame causes demotivation.

Equally, the "you have done well this month, you can go on that course" should also be avoided. Either the person needs to go on the course in order to be better at his or her job, or not. Training budgets are not a "cookie jar" that can be raided to reward somebody. If this happens then training becomes undervalued.

TRAINING AND TRAINING NEEDS ANALYSIS (TNA)

Training as defined in Chapter 2 is much narrower than development and usually refers to a set of specific skills that a person needs for his or her job. Training can occur "on the job," in a company's own training premises, or using external agencies such as local colleges or universities or training consultants used to impart specific skills.

Training costs time and money and it is therefore important that it be carried out in the most cost-effective manner possible. Unfortunately, especially in a recession, it is often training provision that is first in line when expenditure has to be cut. This may be a very short-sighted policy. Many employees see a link between training and recognition by the organization, and the importance of recognition was mentioned in Chapter 1 when referring to the work of Herzberg on motivation – recognition is an important motivator. Organizations that resist cutting their training are likely to be better placed when the economy improves, as they will have better motivated staff equipped with the skills necessary for progress.

This was one of the reasons why British Airways continued to invest in the *Fundamentals of Supervision* program featured in Chapter 5, despite the problems many air-carriers were having during the 1990s. During that period British Airways consistently turned in profits when many of its competitors were posting huge losses.

Benefits

The benefits of a well-trained staff can be summarized as:

» improvements to the existing skills base;
» the provision of a pool of well skilled employees;
» improved operations;
» improved service to internal and external customers;
» increased motivation; and
» retention of skills and experience in the organization.

These are benefits well worth having in any organization and are what makes training and development a good investment.

The training cycle

Fig. 6.1 shows what is known as the ''training cycle''. The ''how'', the ''where'', and the ''who'' of training delivery are discussed later in this chapter.

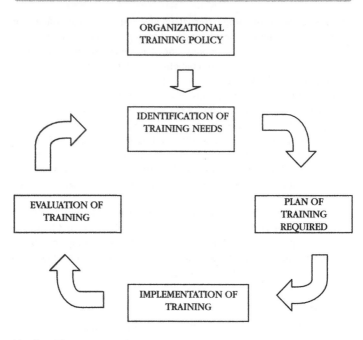

Fig. 6.1 The training cycle.

The aim of training

The aim is to produce learning as defined in Chapter 2 - i.e. a change in behavior and/or attitudes. Before the training person A could do X, after the training A can do X + Y; so learning has occurred, and behavior that could produce only X has been changed to behavior that can do X + Y.

Identification of training needs

A training need may be raised by a line manager as a result of observations or from an appraisal/review interview, or needs may be generated as a result of changes within the organization - a new product, new technology, legislative changes, etc. Any change within a section, a department, or an organization is likely to have training implications and these should be considered whenever changes are contemplated. It is rare for major organizational changes not to have implications for the skills that are needed by the employees.

When deciding training needs, remember that training is not a reward, it should be there to aid both organizational and personal efficiency and effectiveness.

The skills gap

The skills gap is the difference between the skills needed to carry out the required task and the skills the operative or group of operatives actually possesses. Once identified the gap can be filled using a variety of forms of training as discussed below (see Fig. 6.2).

It is an important managerial/supervisory function to identify the skills gap. Training is then the way an organization fills the gap.

PLANNING THE TRAINING

Once a skills gap has been identified then plans need to be made to fill the gap.

Training does not always involve long courses away from the work-place. Training can consist of short sessions on a piece of equipment with the training delivered by the supervisor, manager, or even a more experienced colleague. Many training needs can be met with on-the-job training. Such training was a major component in the salvage of the USS *Lafayette/Normandie* and the building of the "Liberty" ships that is introduced as a case study in Chapter 7.

It is important, however, that those delivering the training understand the nature of the training cycle and have some knowledge of how people learn.

The relationship between the training provider and the organization varies according to the nature of the skills gap and the resources of the organization. Unipart, a UK company featured in another of the case studies in Chapter 7, has invested heavily in training facilities and is able to undertake much of the required training in-house – although outside providers are still used. Some organizations will plan their own training and then ask others to carry it out; large organizations may carry out

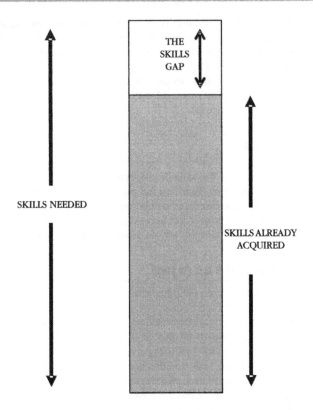

Fig. 6.2 The skills gap.

the vast majority of the cycle, including implementation, while smaller organizations may rely heavily on outside assistance at all stages of the training cycle.

Where an external provider is used there is a need to acquaint that provider with the nature of the skills required, the organizational objectives, and the way the organization operates in order to contextualize the training. Training that is carried out without being contextualized is often less effective than contextualised training; in the case of the latter the trainee can see the relevance to his or her job.

SETTING THE TRAINING OBJECTIVES

The objectives for any training activities should be set using SMART criteria, in that they should be:

» **S**pecific, in that they state exactly what the skills gap is and how it is to be closed.
» **M**easurable, so that at the end of the training it should be possible to quantify the degree of success.
» **A**greed, so that whatever the training need and the way it is met, the trainee and his or her superiors are in agreement about what is needed and how it is to be implemented.
» **R**ealistic, because there is no point in setting a training goal that is beyond the physical or mental capabilities of the trainee. That will guarantee failure and demotivation. Splitting the training up into manageable "chunks" so that success can feed on success is a realistic method of training.
» **T**ime bound, because training should not be open-ended. Trainees and their managers need to know when the training will commence and how long it will last.

In summary

The objectives for training should follow the format below:

» The training need is X.
» The people to be trained are Y.
» At the end of the training they will be able to do . . .
» The following need to agree the training plan: Y + superiors.
» The program is divided up into the following sections . . .
» The training will commence at/on . . .
» The training will last for . . .

IMPLEMENTATION OF THE TRAINING

Psychologists and educationalists have produced many theories of how people learn, many of these theories being the results of animal experiments extrapolated to humans. What is clear, amidst the various theories, is that "practice makes perfect". The more often a person does something, the better he or she is at it – but only up to a point. Familiarity and tiredness can lead to a falling off of performance. This improvement over time is the learning curve that was introduced in Chapter 2.

While success tends to breed success, research shows that a small number of failures, provided that there are some successes, can also act as a motivator. People do learn from failures; but if the number of failures far outweighs successes, the trainee may begin to despair of ever mastering the task. An effective trainer will, at this point, break the task down into even smaller components, if possible, in order to provide the trainee with the opportunity of a small success.

The learning cycle

Adults learn and gain new skills in one of four different ways in which individuals learn. The learning can be enhanced if the right approach is used for different individuals. David Kolb and Roger Fry[1] have developed a model to show how the four types of learning interrelate (Fig. 6.3).

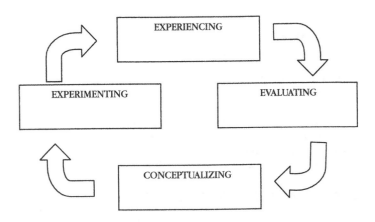

Fig. 6.3 The Kolb learning cycle.

Some people learn best by experiencing the task, then evaluating that experience against their previous knowledge. This leads to the development of a concept that experiments with the task can then confirm or deny. Others are happier learning the theory or concepts, experimenting with these, and using the experiences gained to test (evaluate) their concept, etc.

Kolb and Fry argued that the learning cycle can begin in any one of the four boxes in Fig. 6.3. However, they suggested that the learning process often (but by no means always) begins with a person carrying out a particular action and then seeing the effect of the action in this situation. Following that, the second step is to understand the effect in the particular instance so that if the same action was taken in the same circumstances it would be possible to anticipate what would follow from the action. The third step, understanding the general principle under which the particular instance falls, follows naturally from step two.

When the general principle is understood, the last step is its application through action in a new circumstance within the range of generalization. Once the action is taken, any differences in the effects of the action are noted and evaluated and the conceptualization is modified in the light of the new experience.

Kolb has pointed out that rather than a simple cycle, the model is really a spiral with one cycle leading to another.

Learning styles

The UK workers Alan Mumford and Peter Honey have used Kolb's ideas to produce a typology of learning styles. Learners will use all four of the styles (the styles relate to the Kolb categories) but different types of learner will begin with a different style.

In *Manual of Learning Styles*,[2] Mumford and Honey have looked at which of the Kolb categories different types of people prefer to use to enter the learning cycle. They termed the four types *activists*, *reflectors*, *theorists*, and *pragmatists*.

Activists (Experiencing)

Activists like new experiences; they enter the cycle at the *experiences* stage. They are usually willing to try anything and tend to be enthusiastic about new ideas. They learn best when there are new experiences and problems available, especially where these are short-term results to be gained. They like other people around to bounce ideas off.

Activists tend to leave manuals still in their wrapping – they try things out to see what happens rather than have somebody tell them.

They learn least when learning is passive and involves a great deal of reading or listening to a tutor. They will be more comfortable with more formal learning methods if they have had the opportunity for hands-on experience prior to any seminar or presentations.

Reflectors (Evaluating)

Reflectors like to consider experiences in detail. They tend to be more cautious than activists. While to an activist the experience is everything and evaluation takes second place, to a reflector experiences should be short and then there needs to be plenty of time for evaluation.

Reflectors learn best when they are encouraged to evaluate an activity and then given plenty of time to think about what happened before proceeding to the next task. They learn least when activity follows activity with little or no time to consolidate their thoughts.

Theorists (Conceptualizing)

Theorists like to integrate their observations and experiences into a logical, conceptual framework. They want to know how and why it happened this way. They respond to being given all the details first and then they will try it. In this respect they are the exact opposite of the activist who cannot wait to get his or her hands on the task.

Theorists learn best when they can see how the task fits into the whole and they are directed to the theoretical background to events. They learn least when they are forced to undertake the task before they have understood the implications and theoretical background. They need a clear mental picture before actually undertaking a task.

Pragmatists (Experimenting)

Pragmatists want to try out new theoretical ideas but in practice/simulated activities before moving on to the real thing. They are experimenters. They tend to be very practical people who can make a link between theory and practice but wish to be sure, via experimentation, that their ideas are correct before undertaking the task proper.

Pragmatists learn best when they can concentrate on practical issues and they can see the link between theory and practice. They learn least when they cannot see the relevance between the theory and an immediate practical need.

Learning styles questionnaire

Honey and Mumford have developed a series of questions to ascertain the dominant typology for individuals.[3] It is the dominant typology that determines the start point in the learning cycle. Using the Honey and Mumford terms, the Kolb cycle becomes as shown in Fig. 6.4.

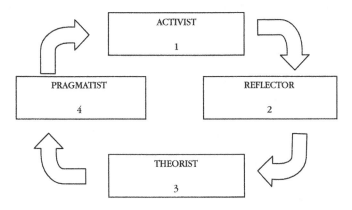

Fig. 6.4 The Kolb learning cycle using Honey and Mumford terms.

» An *activist* begins at 1 and proceeds through 2-3-4 and back to 1.
» A *reflector* begins at 2 and proceeds through 3-4-1 and back to 2.
» A *theorist* begins at 3 and proceeds through 4-1-2 and back to 3.
» A *pragmatist* begins at 4 and proceeds through 1-2-3 and back to 4.

The importance of understanding these styles is that, wherever possible, training should be in the style that best fits the trainee. This is not always possible, especially in group training, but trainers should try to ascertain the preferred style of each trainee in order to use it where possible.

For example, if a person is a theorist the trainer should not say, "Try this to see what happens." That is acceptable for an activist, but a theorist will want to know about the background before trying something new.

Experiential learning

While individuals have different preferred starting points in the learning cycle, it cannot be denied that experience is an important part of the learning process.

The influential US psychologist Carl Ranson Rogers (1902–87) argued that a wish to learn is an innate human characteristic and that there are two categories of learning.[4] The first he called "meaningless learning", which is, for example, the learning of lists by rote; and the second he called "experiential learning", where learning is linked to experience. Most children learn that fires burn the skin through experience no matter how many times they are told beforehand.

There is an old saying that goes "I'll believe it when I see it." This could be paraphrased and turned on its head to represent experiential learning – "I'll learn it when I do it."

The importance of Rogers' work (profiled in Chapter 8) is contained in his belief that significant learning tends to take place when the subject matter is relevant to the personal or work interest of the learner. This is why on-the- job training with an effective coach is so potent (see the next section).

Action learning

Both Rogers in the United States and Revans in the UK have been proponents of "action learning". Stewart and Winters[5] state that action learning is far more than learning-by-doing. The action is in fact not the doing but the responsibility the learner takes for his or her learning.

In an action learning scenario the syllabus is decided by the participants and not by an outside body. This may sound chaotic, but it is adults who are in charge of their own development. The strength of action learning, it is claimed, is the engagement that the learner has with the process, a process that he or she is in charge of. Inputs are contracted in from outside experts but they are not the managers of the learning – that is a role reserved for the learner.

Coaching

As David Logan[6] points out, there is nothing new about coaching. Its basic concepts have been around since human beings began competing in athletic contests, etc. Athletes, especially, have used coaches to guide them through the process of transforming their potential into top performance. Logan argues that business managers face a similar problem – getting maximum performance out of their employees.

Logan believes that there is a two-way payoff for becoming a manager-coach in that the manager and the person being coached both gain new skills and have a better understanding of each other. Logan contends that manager-coaches are more productive, their workplaces are more efficient, their people constantly develop their skills, and their companies' performances improve.

Coaching is a skill that requires a degree of training to acquire. A good understanding of the concept of learning styles is vital for a manager-coach. He or she needs to adapt the coaching style to the learning style of the trainee. The trainee should not have to adapt to the coach.

Coaching is in many ways the modern equivalent to the apprentice-ship system discussed in Chapter 3.

Coaching and Mentoring (Capstone, Oxford) in the ExpressExec series provides further details on coaching.[7]

MONITORING AND EVALUATING THE TRAINING

It can be illuminating to ask people two questions as they embark on a task:

» How will you have succeeded?
» How will you know you have finished?

If the person cannot provide an answer then it is probable that the task has not been thought through properly. Any training plan should have attached to it the success and time criteria.

Andrew Mayo[8] provides a list of the type of measurable goals that can be used to evaluate the success of training and development plans and their implementation. Depending on the reason for the training/development, these include:

» a defined increase in capability – it should be measurable (i.e. can the person now do this?);
» a quantitative (measurable) bottom-line increase – for example a cost saving or increased sales or higher quality and less rejects, or fewer complaints;
» a change in the results of a survey – for example, before the customer-care training 65% of customers were satisfied, after the training 85% expressed satisfaction;
» gaining a qualification (see later); and
» experience in a particular situation.

MULTI-SKILLING

Under the ideas of classical/scientific management developed at the beginning of the twentieth century, workers should be taught just the skills required to carry out their allotted task. In times of stability this may have been effective, but in times of rapid change it is necessary to have employees with a number of skills – hence the concept of multi-skilling.

Multi-skilling provides the organization with a flexible workforce. It also provides the employees with a set of skills that enables them to seek new challenges. Richard Pettinger,[9] the UK writer on both general management and human resource management, makes the point that flexibility, multi-skilling, attitude, expertise, and behavior all feed off each other making for a more effective organization.

Multi-skilling has to be implemented with sensitivity. If employees feel that all that the organization is seeking to achieve is more work for the same pay, then there will be resistance. The concept of multi-skilling needs to be presented in such a manner that the employees can see how their development will benefit from the changes.

DEVELOPMENT

The point was made in Chapter 2 that development is a much longer-term process than training. Development is in many ways akin to growth - slow and steady and yet by the end of the process the person is often very different than he or she was at the beginning. The full benefits of a development program may not be apparent until some time after it has been concluded.

Training is about skills and development is about ideas and attitudes. People do gain new skills in a development process, but they should also acquire the analytical and thinking skills to put what has been learnt into practice.

To give an example, most management development programs include modules on management and financial accounting. A person on the program will acquire some accountancy skills, but of far more importance is the fact that he or she will be able to look at an organization in a different way - by considering its financial position.

The components of a development program fit together like a jigsaw and it may be very near to the end before the whole picture becomes apparent. To use the management development scenario again, one can see how people, finance, information, customers, operations, R&D, etc. fit together to give a complete picture of an organization.

Models of development

Andrew Mayo (quoted earlier) has described a number of development models designed to suit different employee groups. Some of the most important are as follows:

» *A narrow T*. Development is in a specialist, professional field until the person is quite senior in the organization.
» *A wide T*. After a few years of specialist professional develop-ment, those chosen for development have their horizons widened. This type of development usually includes development activities, courses, etc. and time in other parts of the organization in order to gain experience of the whole organization.

» *An I model*. There is a general development at the start of a career, then specialization and then general development much later. Many graduate entry schemes are based on this model where the graduate has a period of time in a number of areas of the organization before specializing. If the person is later deemed suitable for development then he or she may spend time in other areas again.

» *A Y model*. Generalists and specialists have parallel development programs but crossover is not often made.

The Y model is going out of favor, as it does not provide specialists with the opportunities to broaden their horizons.

Growing your own

Organizations that invest in developing employees are growing their own future managers, etc. Some will leave part way through their development and some straight after it. Disillusioned senior managers often use this as an excuse for not providing development. They overlook the fact that others with potential may come to the organization because of the way it develops its staff.

Mentors and mentoring

A mentor shares many of the attributes of a coach – a mentor could be described as a development coach.

The role of a mentor involves working with the person undertaking the development program in order to help clarify ideas and to assist in contextualizing them in the organizational setting. The mentor should also aid the person undergoing development when he or she needs resources from the organization.

A person's mentor should be of sufficient seniority to be able to acquire resources and open doors to aid the development program. The mentor should not have a normal line management relationship with the person. There are things that might be discussed with a mentor that it would be inappropriate to talk about with one's manager. Mentors are there to listen and to advise.

Mentors have been described as like a good uncle or aunt – somebody to look up to and admire but not a parent.

Coaching and Mentoring (Capstone, Oxford) in the ExpressExec series provides further details on mentoring.[10]

COMPETENCE

In a variety of fields there has been a growth in what are known as competence-based programs. In such a program knowledge alone is not enough; the person must show that he or she is competent to perform a task to a set of agreed (often nationally or internationally) criteria. These criteria have three main components:

» what the person must be able to do;
» the range of activities, etc. across which it must be done; and
» the knowledge and understanding that the person needs to possess to be able to transfer the competence.

Consider the simple example of changing a vehicle tire. It is not enough that the person changes one tire – he or she should be able to change front and back tires, to change the tire on a motorcycle, etc. Individuals must also be able to tell their assessors why they are doing what they do, especially where there are safety considerations.

BEST PRACTICE CASE

The European Computer Driving License® (or ECDL) is the European-wide qualification which enables people to demonstrate their competence in computer skills. In fact the qualification is recognized worldwide and is one of the programs offered by TCM in Canada, the subject of the case study in Chapter 4.

Agreed by specialists across Europe, the key benefits stated for the individual are that it:

» raises his or her level of competency in IT and computer skills;
» improves his or her your productivity at home and work;
» requires no prior knowledge of IT or computer skills; and
» provides the individual with a European-wide (and global) industry qualification based on what the individual can do rather than what the person knows about.

The ECDL consists of seven module tests that lead to the qualification. The modules are:

1 Basic concepts of information technology (IT)
2 Using the computer and managing files
3 Word processing
4 Database
5 Spreadsheets
6 Presentation
7 Information and communication

The ECDL is designed specifically for those who wish to gain a basic qualification in computing to help them with their current job, develop their IT skills, and enhance their career prospects. No prior knowledge of IT or computer skills is needed to study the ECDL.

The ECDL syllabus covers the key concepts of computing, practical applications, and their use in the workplace and society in general. It is broken down into the seven modules listed above, each of which must be passed before the ECDL certificate is awarded.

Candidates obtain, usually from a provider, a logbook listing all the modules. As they pass each module, the logbook is signed. The modules may be taken in any order and over any period up to three years – even all at once – offering maximum flexibility. When all the modules have been successfully completed, the logbook is exchanged for a certificate.

THE LEARNING ORGANIZATION

A learning organization is one that taps into the investment it has made in its human capital to assist the whole organization to learn; that is, to produce a change in the organization's behavior. For this to happen everybody in the organization needs to be involved, from the latest new hire to the CEO and the stock/shareholders.

Kline and Saunders[11] provide a clear explanation of what is involved when an organization enters the learning process. Their ten steps are outlined below.

1. Assess the cultural climate for learning in the organization

Learning organizations are not blame cultures. Learning organizations need a culture of honesty and openness.

2. Promote the positive

Learning organizations change and change brings fear. Employees need reassurance about what they are going to have to do and the potential rewards.

3. Make the workplace safe for thinking

Part of any learning process is the articulation of ideas and then bouncing them off those around one. The learning organization needs this type of vibrancy, and this kind of behavior cannot flourish in an atmosphere of cynicism and ridicule. It is worth recalling that Sir Frank Whittle, the first man to propose a working jet engine, had a paper he had written on his ideas while he was a cadet at the Royal Air Force college returned with ''POPPYCOCK'' written across it in red ink!

4. Reward risk-taking

Risks that people take while they are learning should, if they are not too extreme, be rewarded even if there is a failure – provided the person can demonstrate that he or she has learnt from the experience. It is up to the person's manager to set the limits within which risks can be taken. The person who never made a mistake never made anything!

5. Help people to become resources for each other

Earlier in this book the self-help groups that the Open University encouraged were used to indicate how working in a group can aid learning. One of the biggest training and development resources any organization possesses is its people – tap into their experience and encourage them to share it. This was part of the philosophy behind the apprenticeship system.

6. Put power learning to work

Once learning becomes an everyday feature of the organization it will begin to influence the way things are done. Thinks that might have seemed impossible before may now not seem to be so unrealistic.

7. Map out the vision

All organizations need vision. The vision of the learning organizations needs to be disseminated to every person in that organization. Once people know where the organization is going they can see how their role and aspirations fit in.

8. Bring the vision to life

A vision that is not evidenced in the day-to-day actions of the organization is of little use. What happens within the organization should be a reflection of the vision, as training should reflect the needs of the organization.

9. Connect the systems

Organizations (like society) are complex systems. In the next chapter, Unipart in the UK is presented as a training and development success story. In Unipart, as in any learning organization, the learning is diffused throughout the operation. Learning is one of the things that connects the various areas of organizational activity together.

10. Get the show on the road

Although Kline and Saunders present this as their last step to a learning organization, any organization that is at this stage has had the show on the road for quite a long time.

Learning organizations are able to change as circumstances dictate. Too many corporate failures have occurred because the organization as a collection of individuals has been unable to see what is happening – and then, when it is too late, it lacks the human resources for the necessary changes. The learning organization has its human/intellectual capital to draw on.

KEY LEARNING POINTS

» Training and development should be linked to organizational objectives.

» Training and development should never be used as a reward or punishment.

» A training needs analysis (TNA) can help identify the skills gap.

» The training process is a circle or spiral, as described by Kolb's learning cycle.

» People enter the learning cycle at different points depending on their preferred learning style.

» Like any activity, training and development needs to be evaluated against its objectives which should be written in SMART criteria.

» Experiential learning is using experience to support learning.

» Action learning involves the learners managing their own learning process.

» Mentors should be senior but not in a line management relationship with the person undertaking development.

» Competence approaches involve both knowing about and being able to do something.

» Learning organizations have a large resource in their intellectual and human capital.

NOTES

1 David Kolb (1974) *Organizational Psychology*. Prentice Hall, New York.

2 Peter Honey and Alan Mumford (1982) *The Manual of Learning Styles*. P. Honey, Maidenhead.

3 Peter Honey and Alan Mumford (1982) *The Learning Styles Questionnaire*. P. Honey, Maidenhead.

4 See Chapters 8 and 9 for a selection of Rogers' publications.

5 S. Stewart and R. Winter (1995) 'Open and distance learning'. In Truelove, S. (ed.) *The Handbook of Training and Development*. Blackwell, Oxford.

6 David Logan and John King (2001) *The Coaching Revolution*. Adams Media, Holbrook, MA.

7 F. Stone (2002) *Coaching and Mentoring*. Capstone, Oxford.

8 Andrew Mayo (1998) *Creating a Training and Development Strategy*. Chartered Institute of Personnel and Development, London.

9 Richard Pettinger (1998) *Managing the Flexible Work Force*. Cassel, London. See also *Flexible Working* (Capstone, Oxford) in the ExpressExec series.

10 F. Stone (2002) *ibid.*

11 P. Kline and B. Saunders (1998) *Ten Steps to a Learning Organization*, 2nd edn. Great Ocean Publishing, Alexander, NC.

Training and Development Success Stories

The chapter looks at companies and initiatives from the USA, Europe, and Asia that have demonstrated effective training and development programs:

» the US shipbuilding industry during World War II;
» the Unipart group and the Unipart "university"; and
» Canon and its environmental awareness training.

The three case studies in this chapter are very different. The first relates to task-oriented training – possibly the largest training program ever undertaken. The second is focused on a company that provides considerable in-house training and development for its employees. The third looks at a company that provides training to raise awareness of an issue that the company believes is core to its philosophy.

"ROSIE THE RIVETER"

The ExpressExec series is designed for the twenty-first century so it may seem strange to include a case study from the 1940s. It would, however, be remiss in any material on training and development to omit what must rank as one of the most intensive and successful training programs of all time – that of the US shipbuilding industry during World War II.

Prior to 1939 and the outbreak of war in Europe, the United States had been only a minor player in the global shipbuilding industry. At a time when the UK had two vessels of over 80,000 gross registered tonnes (GRT is a measurement of enclosed volume of the ship and not weight) – the *Queen Mary* in service and the *Queen Elizabeth* building on the Clyde in Scotland – and France had the *Normandie* (an 80,000 GRT ship that plays an important part in this story), the largest US-built merchant ship was the 34,000 GRT *America*, then building at Newport News and destined to be a cruise ship during 1940/41 and then until 1946 to be the troop ship USS *West Point*.

The United States had no tradition of large-scale merchant ship-building. Equally there was no tradition of operating a large fleet of merchant ships. The large-scale immigration to the USA in the early years of the twentieth century had been facilitated by British, French, German, and Italian shipping companies. The US involvement in the industry had tended to be financial. It is a little known fact that while the *Titanic* was registered in Britain, had a British crew and appeared completely British, the ship and the White Star Line at the time of the sinking were owned by the Morgan combine – *Titanic* was owned by a US company!

The SS *Normandie* story

The mighty *Normandie* (voted as "Liner of the Century" by the Ocean Liner Society in 2000) was at her berth (Pier 88) on New York's West Side on 3 September 1939, the day Britain and France declared war on Germany following the latter's invasion of Poland on 1 September. She was not to leave that berth as an ocean-going ship again. Her owners the French Line decided that it was safer for the ship to remain in New York so, while the *Queen Mary* and from 1940 the *Queen Elizabeth* were carrying British and Commonwealth troops all over the world, *Normandie* remained in New York.

Following the attack on Pearl Harbor on 7 December 1940, the US government requisitioned *Normandie*, renamed her as the USS *Lafayette*, and began converting the ship to a troopship capable of carrying over 14,000 troops at a time. The conversion required the removal of *Normandie*'s lavish fittings and was almost complete with the ship scheduled to sail to Boston when, on 9 February 1942, sparks from an oxyacetylene cutter that was being used to remove the last of four steel columns in the Grand Lounge set fire to some lifejackets that had been stored there. The lifejackets were filled with kapok and wrapped in oiled paper. The resultant fire was soon out of control.

The United States had only ever operated one large liner – *Leviathan* (54,000 GRT) – that had been the German *Vaterland* until it was awarded to the USA as reparations in 1919. The French Line crew who could have helped fight the fire had long since dispersed, and her designer – the Russian émigré Vladimir Yourkevitch – who was in New York at the time was turned away from the pier and told that the New York Fire Brigade knew what they were doing. They proceeded to pour millions of tons of water onto the ship, water that had no way out of the hull.

The fire was extinguished, but so much water had entered the ship that she began to list. At 2.27 a.m. (EST) on 10 February 1942, *Normandie*, according to eye witnesses, "gently rolled onto her side". The allies had lost a major troop carrier and a New York pier was blocked. While there was no loss of life it was a major disaster for the allied cause and an embarrassment to the New York City Fire Brigade, the US Navy and the US Coast Guard. A well-written novel by Justin Scott has suggested that sabotage was to blame, but an objective analysis seems to point the finger at a set of unfortunate coincidences and a lack of training in operating such a huge vessel.

At the time the United States was busy drafting men into the armed forces and there was not a pool of skilled divers and salvage experts to work on *Normandie*. It was then that US ingenuity and commitment came to the fore. Where was the best place to train as a diver on the *Normandie* operation? – on *Normandie*.

A diving school was established on the side of the ship (the side having become a roof as the ship had turned through 90 degrees. Partnered with more experienced men, the novice divers were trained and learnt as only those who are well motivated can – quickly. In the filthy, dangerous tidal waters of the Hudson River, the superstructure was removed, patches placed over every porthole (scuttle) and opening, and the ship pumped dry. On 15 September 1943 the ship, minus her superstructure and funnels, was afloat again.

Unfortunately the hull had been resting on an outcrop of rock on the riverbed and required major repairs and the engines were ruined. *Normandie* never sailed again and the remains were sold for their scrap value of $3.80 per ton of weight. Nevertheless the USA had shown how quickly a training program could be devised and implemented. It is doubtful whether any country could have managed the task so quickly, and that was only a small part of the mammoth shipbuilding and repairing operation that the United States was to mount as the war progressed.

The full story can be found in *Normandie: Liner of Legend* by Clive Harvey (see Chapter 9).

The Liberty and Victory ships

Admiral Yamamoto, the architect of the Pearl Harbor attack, believed that Japan had to win the war within six months or else the industrial might of the USA would be decisive. While the battles were being fought on distant fronts, a key deciding factor in the outcome of the conflict was which side could outbuild the other in respect of aircraft, ships, tanks, etc.

There was never any real danger of the United States being invaded, and an analysis of the history suggests that Britain was safe from invasion after the Battle of Britain in the Fall of 1940; but that was not known at the time. Britain's major vulnerability lay in her need to import vast quantities of foodstuffs, raw materials, and implements of war manufactured mainly in the USA. The North Atlantic was Britain's main artery. Unbeknown to many, the US Navy had been at war in the North Atlantic since 11 April 1941 when President Roosevelt extended the Pan-American Security Zone well out into the Atlantic (from 60 degrees west to 26 degrees west). On 1 March 1941 the US Navy formed its Support Force Atlantic Fleet with three destroyer squadrons and four squadrons of patrol flying boats to be based in Britain – despite the fact that the USA was not at that time at war with Germany.

Germany's surface raiders (two pocket battleships, two battle-cruisers, and two battleships), while a threat to the Atlantic convoys, achieved very little. In contrast, the German U (*Untersee*) submarines came close to forcing Britain to the brink of disaster just as they had in World War I.

In June 1941, nearly 900,000 tons of allied shipping was sunk in the North Atlantic and a year later in June 1942 the figure had risen to 1.75 million tons in a single month. It was not just the loss of the ships that was such a disaster; survivors were few in the cold waters of the North Atlantic and for every sinking in an eastbound convoy to Britain there was the loss of the ship's valuable cargo.

In 1941 the Allies lost 3.6 million tons of shipping and throughout 1942 losses were a staggering 8.3 million tons of shipping. This meant average losses of 96 merchant ships a month. Britain had begun the war with the world's largest merchant fleet but it was now being decimated. British shipyards were overstretched not only building merchant ships but also the warships necessary to retain a degree of control over the shipping lanes.

Without sufficient merchant hulls to carry the supplies of war across the North Atlantic there could be no liberation of France, and if Britain were forced to surrender through starvation there would be little that the United States could do to attack Germany. Warships may be more glamorous than merchant ships but what was needed was a huge supply of ships capable of a reasonable speed and carrying as much cargo as possible.

The British had designed a simple freighter of about 8000 GRT with reciprocating engines and a speed of about 14 knots – not fast, but as the ships were designed to sail in convoy this speed was acceptable. This design became the "Liberty" ship, one of the five developments that – together with the jeep, the two and a half ton truck, the bulldozer, and the amphibious DUKW – were cited as decisive war winners by General Eisenhower.

What Britain did not possess was the resources to build the ships. The USA had the human resource and the raw materials. The word "manpower" has often been used for human resource, but in the case of the Liberty ships it was also womanpower as women were drafted into the building program in very large numbers.

The program to build the 2700 Liberty ships and their later development the "Victory" ships eventually employed a workforce of 640,000 in shipyards on every coast of the United States. Welding replaced riveting as a means of construction. This was an advantage as it required less physical strength and it was not uncommon to see a diminutive lady welding the plates on an ocean-going freighter. *Rosie the Riveter* became a symbol of America's womanhood going to war. Britain had mobilized a large number of women to work in factories during both world wars but nothing on the scale of the US effort from 1942 to 1945 had ever been seen.

The mobilized workforce was willing but did not have the skills required for engineering tasks. A huge training program that broke the skills down into manageable "chunks" that could be learnt was implemented. Coaching (see Chapter 6), where a new recruit was placed with a more experienced worker, provided valuable on-the-job training.

The skills learnt in the wartime emergency building programs of ships, vehicles, and aircraft meant that in 1945 the USA emerged from the war not only having not been bombed – and thus with its industries intact – but with those industries greatly expanded and possessing a well-trained workforce. Much of the US economic success post-1945 has its roots in wartime emergency programs.

The key to the success lay in the motivation of those who undertook training to aid the armed forces. Willing volunteers with good training make a potent combination. The US Maritime Commission ensured that the disaster of the *Normandie/Lafayette* would not be repeated. Training was given a priority. Those building the ships, tanks, and aircraft were also given morale-boosting talks and visits from the men who would go to war in them. There were public information films showing how Britain benefited from the supplies being sent – not just armaments but foodstuffs for the general population. In the next case study a Unipart group initiative based on quality circles entitled OCC (Our Contribution Counts) is introduced. Part of the training of the workers at Kaiser Shipbuilding and countless other shipyards along the US coastline involved showing the workforce that their contribution did indeed count.

To show what could be done, in a publicity stunt a Liberty ship was completed from keel laying to launch in just 111½ hours. It is said that the paint was still wet as the ship slid down the slipway. A feat like that was a one-off, but the time to build the ships (the learning curve – see Chapter 2) became less and less, month by month. Only a proper training plan that not only provided skills but also aided motivation by ensuring that the worker understood the value of his or her work could have achieved this.

Admiral Yamamoto was right about the industrial strength of the United States. The U-boats were defeated not only by allied warships but also with the development of the mass-produced Liberty ships as the industrial might of the USA ensured that new merchant ships could always be produced at a rate far in excess of losses. In 1943 alone the allies were able to launch 14 million tons of new shipping, outstripping losses by about 11.5 million tons.

Between January and June 1944, one million US soldiers and nearly two million tons of military equipment crossed the Atlantic in preparation for the D-Day Normandy campaign with negligible losses. U-boats continued to harass allied shipping, but they were not to pose a serious threat to the security of Britain for the remainder of the war – in the last 15 months of the war, the allies lost an average of only 12 ships per month. In contrast, the lifespan of a U-boat was reduced to one and a half missions, with 785 of those 1162 built being sunk by the end of the war. In total, U-boats sank 5150 ships during the war.

Designed and built as an expedient, Liberty and Victory ships lasted far longer than had been expected and were seen on the world's oceans well into the final years of the twentieth century. The SS *John W. Brown* is preserved in Baltimore, the SS *Lane Victory* in San Pedro, and the SS *Jeremiah O'Brien* in San Francisco. In 1994 the *Jeremiah O'Brien*, crewed by veterans, passed through the Panama Canal to Portsmouth UK and thence to the D-Day memorial celebrations off the Normandy coast where she was visited by President Clinton.

And as for Rosie the Riveter? Much of the work was in fact welding, not riveting, but whether Rosie was real or not, she was a symbol of what could be achieved and, as such, was as much a part of the training program as the welding sets and instruction manuals.

TIME LINE FOR THE WORLD WAR II BUILDING EFFORT

» **1939**: War breaks out in Europe
» **April 1941**: USA extends Pan-American Security Zone
» **June 1941**: Allied shipping losses in June equal 800,000 + tons
» **December 1941**: Pearl Harbor attacked by Japan; Germany declares war on United States; *Normandie* requisitioned
» **February 1942**: USS *Lafayette* (ex *Normandie*) catches fire and capsizes in New York
» **1942**: US Maritime Commission gears up to build Liberty ships
» **June 1942**: Allied merchant ship losses reach a monthly total of 1.75 million tons
» **September 1943**: USS *Lafayette* raised
» **1943**: The allies lost 3.5 million tons of merchant shipping but launched 14 million tons
» **1945**: Last of 2700 Liberty ships launched
» **1945**: *Normandie* left New York for scrapping
» **1994**: SS *Jeremiah O'Brien* sails from San Francisco to Plymouth UK for D-Day celebrations

KEY INSIGHTS

» It is possible to recruit and train large numbers of workers if they are motivated.
» The training was directly related to the tasks required – hence this was a training program rather than a development opportunity.
» On-the-job training can be very successful, especially with well-motivated employees.
» Splitting the task into manageable "chunks" aids the learning process.
» The learning curve is enhanced if people can see where their tasks fit in.

» Nothing is impossible.
» A symbol such as "Rosie the Riveter" can be a potent icon in training for specific programs.

THE UNIPART GROUP OF COMPANIES (UK)

The Unipart group is one of Europe's leading independent logistics, automotive parts, and accessories companies. Originally a supplier of parts to the automotive plants situated in the Midlands area of the UK around Birmingham, Unipart has grown following a management buyout in 1987 to an organization whose areas of expertise include:

» provision of logistics services to the automotive, IT, mobile communications, defense, and healthcare sectors;
» development and marketing of automotive aftermarket parts;
» manufacture of original equipment (OE) automotive parts;
» supply of truck and trailer components;
» marketing and distribution of caravan, camping, marine parts and accessories;
» supply of rolling stock parts, services, signaling and telecommunications equipment to the rail industry; and.
» provision of consultancy and training to enable sustainable organizational change

The UK car industry has been in a state of flux for many years. Rolls Royce and Bentley are now under German ownership, and the Rover group at the upper end of the mass, family automobile market was also German-owned before BMW divested itself of the brand for the sum of £1 in 2000.

There have always been strong links between Unipart and Rover; indeed Unipart's HQ is in the same area of Oxford as the Rover Cowley plant (previously the main plant of the Morris Motor Company).

As the list of activities above shows, Unipart has not been afraid to diversify, and the group reported profits of $49.6 million (£31 million) in 2000 – a bad year for the UK motor industry – down from $63 million (39.4 million) in 1999. Recovery is, however, under way.

A key feature in Unipart's survival and success is the emphasis placed on training and developing its staff. Unipart was one of the first UK companies to set up its own "university", the Unipart U in 1993. While this is a development not unknown in the USA – as evidenced by the Disney University – it was a bold venture for a UK company. The mission of the Unipart U is to develop, train, and inspire people to achieve world-class performance within the group's companies and amongst its stakeholders.

The Unipart U is the first area seen by any visitor to the group's head office in Oxford. Opened in 1993, the U is an integral part of working life in Unipart – employees enter the U every day on their way to and from work and learn as well as teach in the facility. For a number of years two large teddy bears complete with their own Unipart photo ID badges – Uni Bear and Versity Bear – flanked the reception desk to provide a welcome to the Unipart U. The writer understands that they are now in honorable retirement.

Unipart sees the U as a reflection of the group's intention to train and inspire people to achieve world-class performance and as the platform from which to focus the direction for the future. For Unipart the U is altruistic as it is seen as a route to competitive advantage and a means of preventing skills from becoming obsolete. This makes it an intangible asset, as described in Chapter 2.

There are around 200 different courses running throughout the U facilities that have been developed and are taught by the company's managers and staff. The courses are designed to be practical so that attendees "train for work" and can apply "this morning's learning to this afternoon's job". Courses cover areas such as IT skills, supplier management, team management, customer service, problem solving, and production. The courses are mainly for employees but, increasingly, other stakeholders of the company such as suppliers and customers attend courses and use the facilities.

The U's direction is shaped under the guidance of a "Dean's Group", comprising directors of each of the divisions within the company and chaired by a part-time principal – currently Dan Jones, professor of motor industry management at Cardiff Business School and co-author of *The Machine That Changed The World* and *Lean Thinking*.

The commitment to developing employees has been recognized by the *Investor in People* award, an award that can be gained by UK companies showing that they are investing in the development of their employees.

Unipart U has state-of-the-art facilities. The Learning Curve (the company's resource center) and the Leading Edge (a showroom and training center for new technologies and the latest computer hardware and software) are located next to the reception area at the company's head office. The physical location of training and development in a place where it cannot be missed by visitors and staff alike demonstrates the company's deep commitment to learning and the use of IT to enhance the potential of its people.

Unipart's commitment to continuous learning as a route to competitiveness has been demonstrated through its employee programs (such as OCC circles – Our Contribution Counts – and Mark in Action), through its supplier relationship training activities, and through its investment in training facilities throughout the company's factories and distribution centers around the UK.

Through the Learning Curve facility employees have access to books, audio cassettes, videos, and journals on subjects relevant to the business, as well as reference material including foreign language packs, maps, hotel guides, dictionaries, and encyclopedias. If the information sought is not available the Learning Curve will endeavor to obtain the information required through its links with Templeton College Library and the British Library Document Supply Centre.

As well as full loan facilities and providing access to online information services, the Learning Curve provides study and reading areas where employees can work in peace and quiet, read the daily papers, or watch an instructional video such as "Grapevine" the company's in-house news video. All group employees are members, and temporary and contract personnel can join as associate members.

The next stage of development for the Unipart U has been the Virtual U – an online learning portal for courseware and collaboration. Unipart learning specialists together with information technology experts have developed a managed learning system that can be delivered across any Web-enabled environment.

The Virtual U is a Web-based method of delivering course work, personal development plans, and performance management via the desktop computer. It combines the best aspects of Web learning with the leading edge techniques for knowledge management. The Virtual U has led to a partnership with 11 local colleges and universities to develop an Oxfordshire Virtual Campus. Unipart has always been aware of its role as a local employer and has worked in partnership with other training providers since 1987.

Through this online university structure, employees can enroll for courses that are delivered direct to their personal computer anywhere and at any time in a similar manner to the TCM programs described in Chapter 4. Online courses are from 15 minutes in length to multiple modules that run for more than an hour in total. Within the structure of each learning module is the ability to deliver fast feedback to the user. The user is notified of concepts that may not be fully understood and is given a rating for the quantifiable amount of knowledge that he or she has received during an online learning session.

This virtual learning environment provides individuals with the opportunity to access learning at their workplace, from home or in any other environment that allows them to dial up the Virtual U. Individuals can learn at their own pace and can access learning material when they need it on a "just in time" basis. The Virtual U also enables users to share information electronically with colleagues or to engage in Internet-based tutorial sessions with leading experts in their field of endeavor.

The use of IT in advanced communications techniques on a corporate scale is an indication of the power of computing in freeing the creative spirit and enthusiasm in all employees. In the early 1990s, Unipart recognized the importance of integrating IT not just into the business processes, but also into the very culture of the company.

In 1994 the Leading Edge, a technology-training center, was opened to reduce what Unipart has described as "the level of techno-fear" in its employees. As techno-fear has receded as people become more familiar with the technology, the Leading Edge facility has evolved into a showroom for the latest technological developments in hardware and software where employees can drop in during any time of the day to try new software packages, explore new techniques such as multimedia and PC conferencing, or simply learn to surf the Internet.

Unipart's latest training and development concept is the "Faculty on the Floor" through which employees can work on production-related problems using computer-based problem-solving tools and best-practice Websites from training facilities located on the shop floor. The aim is to improve quality, increase productivity, and reduce costs continually. This concept has been developed as a direct extension of the Unipart U to bring learning directly onto the shop floor. It enables individual employees to develop the key knowledge and skills that they need to improve quality and productivity in their day-to-day jobs. It also enables teams to tackle production situations using problem-solving circles, and then to use their learning by implementing new ideas or innovations right on the production line.

UNIPART TIME LINE

- **1987**: Management buyout
- **1993**: Opening of Unipart U
- **1997**: Pilot of Faculty on the Floor
- **1998**: Faculty on the Floor implemented company-wide; OCC (the Unipart version of quality circles) provided with a dedicated Web site to allow ideas to flow throughout the group; Leading Edge facility expanded to allow non-PC users and owners in the organization to access the Internet
- **2000**: Development of the Virtual U and the Oxfordshire Virtual Campus

KEY INSIGHTS

- Training and development is an integral part of gaining competitive advantage.
- Both training and development opportunities are provided.
- There is management commitment to providing world-class training facilities.
- Training and development are seen as a part of the organization's business, not a nice-to-have-if-we-can-afford-it extra.

> » Training and development are linked to the shop floor.
> » There are partnerships with colleges and universities.

CANON (JAPAN)

The name of the Japanese electronics company Canon is known throughout the world for a range of cameras, photocopiers, printers, etc.

The corporate philosophy of Canon is *kyosei*, meaning living and working together for the common good. In an attempt to play its part in developing *kyosei*, not just in Japan but also in the countries where its products are sold, Canon believes it should establish good relations, not only with its customers and the communities in which they operate, but also with nations, the environment, and the natural world.

This involves considering the level of environmental management and undertaking environmental activities to contribute to the society. In order to achieve this Canon has embarked upon a program to raise the awareness of all employees regarding the importance of the environment and to encourage them to take the necessary environmental measures at the workplace and at home. In Japanese culture there are not the clear distinctions between work and home prevalent in the West.

Canon's products are high tech but use toners, films, inks, etc. that could have a detrimental effect on the environment, as can waste products from the manufacturing process. Canon is aware of this and devotes considerable effort to raising environmental awareness.

In order to train personnel to lead environmental activities at operational sites and workplaces, Canon offers environmental education to employees of different ranks and provides a variety of programs and seminars to nurture environmental specialists, and encourages employees to participate in external lectures and training programs.

The environmental program commenced in 1996 and covers new hires and training for existing staff on a global basis. In 1996, 2000 employees undertook the environmental training – a figure that rose to 10,000 in the year 2000. Much of the training is in-house but there are external seminars and other activities that employees can attend.

This commitment to the environment may be costly, but Canon is so wedded to the concept of *kyosei* that any cutting back on training for environmental awareness would be seen as a breach of the company's core philosophy.

A major aim of the company is to reduce the environmental burden throughout a product's life cycle. For this reason it is important to incorporate environmental features at the design stage. From 2000, Canon has provided training on the important areas of Design for Environment for engineers and technicians mainly from the development and production departments. These seminars were so well received that the number was increased for 2001.

In order to enhance the environmental awareness of staff, environmental showrooms were set up at Canon's headquarters and a number of manufacturing plants. These showrooms exhibited the unique activities of the particular facility and were thus of direct relevance to the workforce at the plant.

In 1998 Canon began to host technology forums to upgrade and develop the technological level of the Canon group of companies. These forums are used to present the latest technology and specific products. Recently the focus has been on recycling-related technologies.

This type of training – which may not have a direct relation to the financial bottom line but which reflects the company's values – is a new development in training but an important one. On a fragile planet with limited resources and a growth of "green" issues and pressure groups, care for the environment may well be a key to survival. Employees who care about waste and waste management are much less likely to produce as much waste as those who do not understand the environmental concerns. Hence such training may well improve the bottom line in the medium to long term.

CANON TIME LINE

» **1933**: Precision Optical Instrument Laboratory founded
» **1934**: Canon trademark adopted
» **1947**: Name changed to Canon Camera Co.
» **1969**: Named changed to Canon Inc.
» **1996**: Environmental training program begun with 2000 trainees

- **1997**: Number of trainees increased to 3000
- **1998**: Number of trainees increased to 4500; technology forums begun
- **1999**: Number of trainees increased to 6000
- **2000**: Number of trainees increased to 10,000; Design for Environment training commences

KEY INSIGHTS

- Training is not directly related to the tasks but to a part of the organization's cultural beliefs.
- Large numbers of staff are involved.
- Training has been progressive in that new initiatives have been added.
- The organization believes that it has a duty to provide training in organizational awareness.

Key Concepts and Thinkers

» Glossary of terms.
» Related concepts and thinkers.

A GLOSSARY FOR TRAINING AND DEVELOPMENT

Action learning – a system for adult development whereby the learner(s) take responsibility for the learning process producing their own syllabus, etc.

Coaching – the process in which a more experienced person works on a one-to-one basis with a less experienced one to improve the latter's performance.

Competencies – a set of agreed standards that detail tasks a person should be able to undertake, the range of situations to which they apply, and the knowledge and understanding that relates to them.

Computer-assisted learning (CAL) – the use of a computer to train people in tasks using simulations, questioning, etc.

Computer-based training (CBT) – similar to CAL but with a wider, more developmental focus.

Continuous professional development (CPD) – the requirement that many professions and jobs have for ongoing training and development to enable the individual to work with new technologies and systems.

Culture – the values, attitudes, and beliefs ascribed to and accepted by a group, nation or organization; in effect, "the way we do things around here."

Development – a process in which learning occurs through experience and where the results of the learning enhance not only the task skills of the individual but also his or her attitudes.

Education – the broadening of the knowledge and skills base of the individual and indeed the group with the objective of the individual functioning in and being a benefit to the society he or she lives in.

European Computer Driving License (ECDL) – a set of standards for a basic qualification in computer use; known as the ICDL (International Computer Driving License) outside Europe.

Grudge purchase – Something that is necessary but for which payment is begrudged (e.g. insurance and healthcare). Training is sometimes considered as a grudge purchase by less enlightened organizations.

Home working – employees who work from home using ICT as a means of keeping in touch with their base.

Human/intellectual capital – the asset value of the knowledge and experience of the employees of an organization

Information and communication technology (ICT) – technology related to the connection of computer and communications technology to produce a synergy (see below) between them. ICT was originally known as IT (information technology). However, more and more computer-type applications also involve communication with other computers or communication devices – hence the adoption of the acronym ICT.

Intangible assets – assets that cannot be touched or seen but are nevertheless valuable – such as the knowledge base of an organization.

International Computer Driving License (ICDL) – the name given to the European Computer Driving License outside Europe.

Learning – the process by which behavior and attitudes are changed.

Learning curve – the improvement in performance of a task over time.

Learning cycle – a four-stage model consisting of experiencing, evaluating, conceptualizing, and experimenting.

Learning styles – a person's dominant learning style determines the point at which he or she enters the learning cycle (above). There are four styles: activists, reflectors, theorists, and pragmatists.

Mentoring – the process whereby an experienced person (other than the individual's manager) provides counsel and guidance to assist the individual in his or her organizational growth.

Skills gap – the gap between the skills a person has and the skills that he or she needs to carry out a task.

Synergy – a phenomenon where the sum of the parts is greater than the whole. A computer and a camera connected to a telephone can aid communication far more than might be expected by examining the individual capabilities of the three components.

Telecottage – a central point usually in a remote area that is equipped with ICT facilities and which acts as a base for a group of home workers or trainees.

Training – specific instruction concerned with the mastering of a particular task or set of tasks.

Training cycle – the process of the identification of training needs, the implementation of training, the evaluation of the training, and any further training needs that become apparent in line with the organization's training policies.

Training needs analysis (TNA) – a systematic review of the current skills base against organizational requirements in order to identify the skills gap.

KEY THINKERS

All of the books referred to in this section are listed fully in Chapter 9.

Peter Honey

A highly respected name in training and development, Peter Honey together with Alan Mumford are best known for their work on learning styles covered in Chapter 6. The tests that they have developed to ascertain an individual's preferred learning style – and thus his or her optimum point of entry into the learning cycle – are used across the globe.

Of Peter Honey's 50+ major publications (a number of which are published by his own publishing company), the most relevant to the topic in this material are listed below.

Notable publications

» *The Manual of Learning Styles* (with Alan Mumford), 1982
» *The Learning Styles Questionnaire* (with Alan Mumford), 1982
» *Using Your Learning Styles* (with Alan Mumford), 1986
» *The Manual of learning Opportunities* (with Alan Mumford), 1986
» *The Opportunist Learner* (with Alan Mumford), 1990
» *Face to Face Skills*, 1990
» *How to Manage Your Learning*, 1996
» *Peter Honey's 21 Questionnaires for Personal Development*, 2000
» *Learning Log: a Way to Enhance Learning from Experience*, 2000

Peter Klein

Peter Klein, based in South Bend, Indiana, has pioneered methods of accelerated learning that have been used both by trainers and by schoolteachers. Together with Bernard Saunders, Klein has produced

Ten Steps to a Learning Organization – a practical guide that can be contextualized to fit specific organizational needs.

Klein has been a promoter of innovative learning methods and in addition to his non-fiction works is also an accomplished fiction writer.

Notable publications

» *School Success: the Inside Story*, 1992
» *Ten Steps to a Learning Organization* (with Bernard Saunders), 1993
» *Why America's Children Can't Think*, 2002

David Kolb

David A. Kolb is professor of organizational behavior at the Weatheread School of Management, which he joined in 1976. Born in 1939, Kolb received his higher education at Knox College and Harvard in 1967. Besides his work on experiential learning, Kolb is also known for his contribution to thinking around organizational behavior with interests in the nature of individual and social change, experiential learning, career development, and executive and professional education.

Working with Roger Fry, Kolb created his famous model out of four elements: concrete experience, observation and reflection, the formation of abstract concepts, and testing in new situations. He represented these in the famous experiential learning cycle discussed in Chapter 6. In his work he has argued that the learning cycle can begin at any one of the four points – and that it should really be approached as a continuous spiral. However, he has suggested that the learning process often begins with a person carrying out a particular action and then seeing the effect of the action in this situation. Following this, the second step is to understand these effects in the particular instance so that if the same action were taken in the same circumstances it would be possible to anticipate what would follow from the action. In this pattern the third step would be understanding the general principle under which the particular instance falls.

Notable publications

» *Organizational Psychology*, 1974
» *Changing Human Behavior* (with Ralph K. Schwitzgebel), 1974

» *Organizational Behavior*, 6th edn (with Joyce Osland and Irwin Rubin), 1991
» *The Organizational Behavior Reader*, 6th edn (with Joyce Osland and Irwin Rubin), 1995

David Logan

A professor at the University of Southern California, Logan, together with ex-athlete John King, is a keen advocate of coaching as a component of empowerment.

The basic concepts of coaching have been around since human beings began competing. Athletes use coaches to guide them through the process of transforming their potential into top performance, and business managers face a similar problem – getting maximum performance out of employees. Logan believes that the payoff for becoming a manager-coach is clear: manager-coaches are more productive, their workplaces are more efficient, their people constantly develop their skills, and their companies' performances improve.

Notable publication
» *The Coaching Revolution* (with John King), 2001

Andrew Mayo

Originally a chemistry graduate, Andrew Mayo is an international consultant in human resource management and organizational development. Much of his work is involved with ensuring that the training and development process meets the needs both of the organization and the trainee.

Mayo spent 30 years working for major international companies (he was the director of human resource development at International Computers Ltd – ICL) and so is able to blend practice and theory.

Mayo is especially interested in the value of intellectual capital and how this can be developed with an approach to training and development that balances organizational and individual needs.

Notable publications
» *Managing Careers*, 1991
» *The Power of Learning* (with Elizabeth Lank), 1994

» *Motivating People in Lean Organizations* (with Linda Holbeche), 1997
» *Creating a Training and Development Strategy*, 1998
» *Managing Career Development*, 1999
» *Human Value of Enterprise: Valuing People as Assets*, 2001

Alan Mumford

Working closely with Peter Honey (q.v.) and developing the leaning styles with him, Alan Mumford has been involved with the learning process in adults and in the workplace for many years. In addition to the works written with Honey he is also the author of a number of internationally used texts relating to training and development, especially in the fields of management development and action learning.

Notable publications

» *Making Experience Pay*, 1980
» *Manager and Training*, 1981
» *The Manual of Learning Styles* (with Peter Honey), 1982
» *The Learning Styles Questionnaire* (with Peter Honey), 1982
» *Using Your Learning Styles* (with Peter Honey), 1986
» *The Manual of Learning Opportunities* (with Peter Honey), 1986
» *Learning to Learn for Managers*, 1986
» *Action Learning*, 1987
» *Developing Top Managers*, 1988
» *The Opportunist Learner* (with Peter Honey), 1990
» *Management Development*, 1991
» *How Managers Can Develop Managers*, 1993
» *Learning at the Top*, 1995
» *Effective Learning*, 1995

Reg Revans

Reg Reevans is considered the most influential UK authority on the concept of action learning. He has been very much concerned with the concept that learning is the restructuring and reordering of knowledge and then applying those changes to the situations one finds oneself in.

Quality circles (or the Unipart Our Contribution Counts groups – see Chapter 7) are an example of where a group can apply action learning.

In action learning the agenda is set by the learners themselves and they then "buy in" external expertise when necessary if it does not exist within the group.

Notable publications

» *Developing Effective Managers*, 1971
» *Action Learning*, 1980
» *Origins and Growth of Action Learning*, 1982
» *ABC of Action Learning*, 1998

Carl Ransom Rogers

Carl Rogers was an American psychologist and the founder of "client-centered" or "non-directed" psychotherapy, a widely influential, humanistic approach. Rogers also made significant contributions to the field of adult education with his experiential theory of learning.

During his career Rogers held professorships at the University of Rochester, Ohio State University, University of Chicago, and the University of Wisconsin. Later he was the founder and resident fellow at the Center for Studies of the Person, La Jolla, California.

Rogers maintained that all human beings have a natural desire to learn. He defined two categories of learning: meaningless/cognitive learning and significant, or experiential.

According to Rogers, the role of the teacher is to facilitate experiential learning by:

» setting a positive climate for learning;
» clarifying the purposes of the learner(s);
» organizing and making available learning resources;
» balancing intellectual and emotional components of learning; and
» sharing feelings and thoughts with learners but not dominating.

With regard to the personal growth and development of the learner, Rogers suggests:

1. Significant learning takes place when the subject matter is relevant to the personal interests of the student.

2. Learning which is threatening to the self (e.g. new attitudes or perspectives) is more easily assimilated when external threats are at a minimum.
3. Learning proceeds faster when the threat to the self is low.
4. Self-initiated learning is the most lasting and pervasive.

Notable publications

» *On Becoming a Person*, 1961
» *Freedom to Learn*, 1969
» *Freedom to Learn for the Eighties* (a thorough revision of *Freedom to Learn*), 1983
» *The Carl Rogers Reader: Selections from the Lifetime Work of Carl Rogers*, 1989

Bernard Saunders

Bernard Saunders worked with Peter Kline (q.v.) on *Ten Steps to a Learning Organization*. Like Kline, Saunders has been involved with innovative methods of training and development, working with many Fortune 500 companies while consulting in the areas of organizational change.

Notable publication

» *Ten Steps to a Learning Organization* (with Peter Kline), 1993

Resources for Training and Development

This chapter is concerned with where to find resources for the study of training and development: books, serials, and Websites.

The American Management Association (AMA) is the world's leading membership-based management development organization. AMA offers a full range of business education and management development programs for individuals and organizations in Europe, the Americas, and Asia. Through a variety of seminars and conferences, assessments and customized learning solutions, books and online resources, more than 700,000 AMA members and customers a year learn superior business skills and best management practices from a faculty of top practitioners. The online facilities offer access to a wide range of articles including issues related to training and development. [www.amanet.org]

BOOKS

Dates of books in this chapter may differ from those shown in earlier chapters. The dates here are of editions that have been revised from the date of first publication, as shown in the chapter material.

» Cartwright, R. (2001) *Managing Diversity*. Capstone, Oxford.
» Cartwright, R. (2002) *Going Global*. Capstone, Oxford.
» Churchill, W.S. (1930) *My Early Life*. Fontana, London.
» Davies, C. (1997) *Divided by a Common Language*. Mayflower Press, Sarasota, FL.
» Harris, P.R. and Moran, R.T. (2000) *Managing Cultural Differences*. Gulf Publishing, Houston, TX.
» Herzberg, F. (1962) *Work and the Nature of Man*. World Publishing, New York.
» Honey, P. (1990) *Face to Face Skills*. Gower, London.
» Honey, P. (1996) *How to Manage Your Learning*. P. Honey, Maidenhead.
» Honey, P. (2000) *Peter Honey's 21 Questionnaires for Personal Development*. P. Honey, Maidenhead.
» Honey, P. (2000) *Learning Log: a Way to Enhance Learning from Experience*. P. Honey, Maidenhead.
» Honey, P. and Mumford, A. (1982) *The Manual of Learning Styles*. P. Honey, Maidenhead.

» Honey, P. and Mumford, A. (1982) *The Learning Styles Questionnaire*. P. Honey, Maidenhead.
» Honey, P. and Mumford, A. (1986) *Using Your Learning Styles*. P. Honey, Maidenhead.
» Honey, P. and Mumford, A. (1986) *The Manual of learning Opportunities*. P. Honey, Maidenhead.
» Honey, P. and Mumford, A. (1990) *The Opportunist Learner*. P. Honey, Maidenhead.
» Irving, C. (1993) *Wide Body: the Making of the Boeing 747*. Hodder & Stoughton, London.
» Joynt, P. and Morton, R. (eds) (1999) *The Global HR Manager*. Chartered Institute of Personnel and Development, London.
» Kline, P. (1992) *School Success: the Inside Story*. Great Ocean Publishing, Alexander, NC.
» Kline, P. (2002) *Why America's Children Can't Think*. Inner Ocean Publishing, Alexander, NC.
» Kline, P. and Saunders, B. (1993) *Ten Steps to a Learning Organization*. Great Ocean Publishing, Alexander, NC.
» Kolb, D.A. (1974) *Organizational Psychology*. Prentice Hall, New York.
» Kolb, D.A. and Schwitzgebel R.K. (1974) *Changing Human Behavior*. Prentice Hall, New York.
» Kolb, D.A., Osland, S. and Rubin, Irwin M. (1991) *Organizational Behavior*, 6th edn. Prentice Hall, New York.
» Kolb, D.A., Osland, S. and Rubin, Irwin M. (1995) *Organizational Behavior Reader*, 6th edn. Prentice Hall, New York.
» Lessem, R. (1990) *Developmental Management*. Blackwell, Oxford.
» Lewis, R.D. (1999) *Cross Cultural Communications: a visual Approach*. Transcreen, London.
» Logan, D. and King, J. (2001) *The Coaching Revolution*. Adams Media, Holbrook, MA.
» Maslow, A. (1970) *Motivation and Personality*. Harper & Row, New York.
» Mayo, A. (1991) *Managing Careers*. Chartered Institute of Personnel and Development, London.

» Mayo, A. (1998) *Creating a Training and Development Strategy*. Chartered Institute of Personnel and Development, London.
» Mayo, A. (1999) *Managing Career Development*. Fenman Training, London.
» Mayo, A. (2001) *Human Value of Enterprise: Valuing People as Assets*. Nicholas Brealey, London.
» Mayo, A. and Holbeche, L. (1997) *Motivating People in Lean Organizations*. Butterworth–Heinemann, Oxford.
» Mayo, A. and Lank, E. (1994) *The Power of Learning*. Chartered Institute of Personnel and Development, London.
» Mumford, A. (1971) *Manager and Training*. Pitman, London.
» Mumford, A. (1980) *Making Experience Pay*. McGraw-Hill, London.
» Mumford, A. (1986) *Learning to Learn for Managers*. MCB University Press, Bradford.
» Mumford, A. (1987) *Action Learning*. MCB University Press, Bradford.
» Mumford, A. (1988) *Developing Top Managers*. Gower, London.
» Mumford, A. (1991) *Management Development*. Chartered Institute of Personnel and Development, London.
» Mumford, A. (1993) *How Managers can Develop Managers*. Gower, London.
» Mumford, A. (1995) *Learning at the Top*. McGraw-Hill Europe, London.
» Mumford, A. (1995) *Effective Learning*. Chartered Institute of Personnel and Development, London.
» Nicholson, M. (2000) *Managing the Human Animal*. Crown, New York.
» Pettinger, R. (1998) *Managing the Flexible Work Force*. Cassel, London.
» Revens, R. (1971) *Developing Effective Managers*. Longman, London.
» Revens, R. (1980) *Action Learning*. Blond & Briggs, London.
» Revens, R. (1982) *Origins and Growth of Action Learning*. Chartwell & Bratt, Bromley.
» Revens, R. (1998) *ABC of Action Learning*. Lemos & Crane, London.
» Rogers, C. (1969) *Freedom to Learn*. Prentice Hall, New York.

» Rogers, C. (1983) *Freedom to Learn for the Eighties: a Thorough Revision of Freedom to Learn*. Charles Merril, New York.

» Rogers, C. (1989) *The Carl Rogers Reader: Selections from the Lifetime Work of Carl Rogers*. Constable, New York.

» Rogers, C. (1990) *On Becoming A Person*. Constable Robinson, New York.

» Stauffer, D. (2000) *Business the AOL Way*. Capstone, Oxford.

» Stewart, S. and Winter, R. (1995) 'Open and distance learning'. In Truelove, S. (ed.) *The Handbook of Training and Development*. Blackwell, Oxford.

» Stone, F. (2002) *Coaching and Mentoring*. Capstone, Oxford.

» Thomson, R. (1959) *The Psychology of Thinking*. Penguin, London.

» Trompenaars, F. (1993) *Riding the Waves of Culture*. Economist Books, London.

For information about Liberty and Victory ships and the *Normandie*/USS *Lafayette*

» Bunker, J.G. (1973) *Liberty Ships*. Naval Institute, Washington.

» Cooper, S. (1997) *Liberty Ship: the Voyages of the John W. Brown, 1942–1946*. Naval Institute Press, Washington.

» Harvey, C. (2001) *Normandie: Liner of Legend*. Tempus Publishing, Stroud.

» Sawyer, L.A. and Mitchell, W.H. (1985) *The Liberty Ships*. LLP Professional Publishing, London.

» Scott, J. (1981) *Normandie Triangle* [in US] and *The Man Who Loved the Normandie* [in UK]. Granada, New York and London.

SERIALS

Adults Learning

The journal of the UK National Institute of Adult Continuing Education (NIACE) published 10 times a year. It is a forum for debate on all issues affecting policy and practice in adult learning. Each issue contains an editorial commentary, a news section on events and activities in the UK and beyond, a variety of articles, and a book reviews section. [www.niace.org.uk]

Career Development International

A UK-based journal that provides an international forum for all those who wish to gain a greater understanding of career development and its associated issues. It forms an arena for academics to share information and ideas that will help them examine the links between individual career progression and organizational needs. [www.emeraldinsight.com/cdi.htm]

Harvard Business Review

A leading business and management resource. It is read worldwide and features contributions by the leading names in business and management. Published 10 times a year and available by subscription. [www.hbsp.harvard.edu/products/hbr]

Human Resource Development Quarterly

A journal published by John Wiley in the United States and focusing directly on the evolving field of human resource development (HRD). The journal has become a major forum for interdisciplinary exchange on the subject of HRD. [www.interscience.wiley.com/jpages]

Human Resource Management International Digest

A digest of useful HR articles from many sources gathered on a global basis and published seven times a year. Available on subscription. [www.mcb.co.uk/hrmid]

HR Magazine

An HR magazine covering a wide range of issues and published by the Society for Human Resource Management in Alexandria, VA. [www.shrm.org]

Industry and Higher Education

Published six times per year in the United States, this journal is dedicated to the relationships between business and industry and higher education institutions. With a strong emphasis on practical aspects, the journal covers organizational, economic, political, legal, and social issues relating to developments in education–industry collaboration. Among the key topics are:

» technology transfer from research to commercial application;
» preparing students for the world of work;
» international and national initiatives for collaboration;
» respective needs in the industry–education relationship;
» lifelong learning;
» funding of higher education;
» educating for entrepreneurship;
» university–industry training programs;
» business–education partnerships for social and economic progress;
» skills needs and the role of higher education;
» formation, structure and performance of academic spin-off companies;
» academic accreditation for workplace learning;
» personnel exchange;
» industrial liaison in universities;
» intellectual property in the HE sector; and
» distance education.

[www.ippublishing.com/general_industry.asp]

International Journal of Human Resource Management

A journal that is concerned with strategic human resource management and future trends in a global environment. Published eight times a year by Routledge and available on subscription. [www.tandf.co.uk/journals/routledge]

International Journal of Training and Development

This journal provides an international forum for the reporting of high-quality research, analysis, and debate for the benefit of the academic and corporate communities, as well as those engaged in public policy formulation and implementation. Multi-disciplinary, international, and comparative, the journal publishes research which ranges from the theoretical, conceptual, and methodological to more policy-oriented types of work. The journal reports on academic work which specifies and tests the explanatory variables which may be related to training. [www.blackwellpublishers.co.uk]

Journal of Career Development

Published by Kluwer Academic in New York, this journal provides the professional, the public, and policymakers with the latest in career development theory, research, and practice, while focusing on the impact of theory and research on practice. Among the topics covered are career education, adult career development, career development of special needs populations, and career and leisure. [www.kluweronline.com]

Journal of Management Development

Produced ten times a year, the journal explores the concepts, models, tools, and processes which companies are using to help their managers become better equipped to tackle the challenges and opportunities of change. Coverage includes:

» competence-based management development;
» developing leadership skills;
» developing women in management;
» global management;
» the new technology of management development;
» team building;
» organizational development and change; and
» performance appraisal.

[www.emeraldinsight.com]

Management Today

Published by the Institute of Management in the UK, monthly to members or by subscription. It often contains useful articles on issues concerned with training and especially with management development. The Institute also provides management development programs in association with approved providers. [www.inst-man.org.uk]

Organizational Behavior and Human Decision Processes

Published in San Diego by Academic Press for a global academic market, this journal is concerned with organizational behavior, organizational psychology, and human cognition, judgment, and decision-making; hence its relevance to training and development. The journal features articles that present original empirical research, theory development, literature reviews, and methodological advancements relevant to the areas above. Topics covered include perception, attitudes, emotion, well-being, motivation, choice, and performance. [www.academicpress.com/obhdp]

People Management

Magazine of the UK Chartered Institute of Personnel and Development (CIPD). Contains articles on all aspects of personnel and training with special relevance to the UK. Available by subscription and published every two weeks. [www.peoplemanagement.co.uk]

Training Journal

A UK-based monthly journal that was originally founded as *Training Officer* in 1965 and was the official publication of the Institute of Training Officers. The journal's aim is to deliver informative, timely, and practical content to assist anyone involved in workplace learning, training, and development. Both Peter Honey and Andrew Mayo (see Chapter 8) write regular columns for the journal. [www.trainingjournal.co.uk]

Training Magazine

A professional development magazine, published in Minneapolis, that advocates training and workforce development as a business tool. The magazine delves into management issues such as leadership and succession planning, HR issues such as recruitment and retention, and training issues such as learning theory, on-the-job skills assessments, and aligning core workforce competencies to enhance the bottom line impact of training and development programs. Written for training, human resources and business management professionals in all industries. Editorials includes best practice case studies for a wide range of business challenges, investigative analyses of training's strategic applications within leading global organizations, and in-depth research. [www.trainingsupersite.com/training]

WEBSITES

» American Management Association: www.amanet.org
» Caltech (CIT): www.caltech.edu
» Canon: www.canon.com
» *Harvard Business Review*: www.hbsp.harvard.edu/products/hbr
» Institute of Management (UK): www.inst-mgt.org.uk
» *International Journal of Human Resource Management*: www.tandf.co.uk/journals/routledge
» MIT: www.mit.edu
» *People Management*: www.peoplemanagement.co.uk
» SS *Jeremiah O'Brien*: www.geocities.com/jeremiahobrien/obrien.html
» SS *John W Brown*: www.libertyships.com
» SS *Lane Victory*: www.lanevictory.com
» TCM: www.tcm.com
» Unipart: www.unipart.co.uk
» University of Manchester Institute of Science and Technology: www.umist.ac.uk
» University of the Highlands and Islands Millennium Institute: www.uhi.ac.uk

Ten Steps to Effective Training and Development

The 10 steps to effective training and development are, in summary:

1 View training and development as an investment.
2 Match training and development to organizational objectives.
3 Assess training needs in consultation with the potential trainee and the line manager.
4 Grow your own.
5 Don't treat training as a punishment.
6 Use learning styles to enhance the training and development process.
7 Put a monitoring and evaluation procedure in place.
8 Remember that learning never stops.
9 Structure the training.
10 Do not try to impose development.

1. VIEW TRAINING AND DEVELOPMENT AS AN INVESTMENT

It cannot be denied that there are costs to training and development – costs in both money and time. However, as training and development increase the intellectual capital of the organization and also make it more efficient and productive, the medium- to long-term benefits far outweigh the costs. Staff are likely to be more motivated and the organization is likely to attract applications from people who want to make their long-term future with it.

In common with every other investment that an organization makes, it is important to ensure that it is providing the required return; hence the importance of monitoring and evaluation.

2. MATCH TRAINING AND DEVELOPMENT TO ORGANIZATIONAL OBJECTIVES

No organization should undertake any activity unless it can be shown that the activity is in pursuit of an organizational goal. Training and development are no different.

The most wonderful training and development programs may be on offer but they should be used only if the content of the programs can be shown to relate to the organization's objectives.

Individuals who wish to be sponsored by the organization through the provision of time and/or money should accept that the organization may well not wish to sponsor programs that are unconnected with its objectives. It may be that an organization will sponsor an employee to undertake a general degree (BA, etc.) in the belief that this will make the employee more rounded and with better general schemes as well as acting as a motivator. This is perfectly acceptable provided there are resources available. However, if resources are tight then priority should be given to training and development that is work-related.

3. ASSESS TRAINING NEEDS IN CONSULTATION WITH THE POTENTIAL TRAINEE AND THE LINE MANAGER

There is nothing worse as a manager than finding out that a member of your team is undergoing training and development and you knew nothing about it. This should not occur in an efficient organization as the training and development should, as covered above, be linked to the organization's objectives.

Early consultation with a person's manager allows the two of them to discuss time off, extra resources, and how the manager can provide opportunities for the individual to practice new skills within the work situation.

Individuals should never be told "You are going on this program". A person's training and development should be discussed with the individual. The person can then plan his or her time and activities around the training and development and can seek advice and resources from their colleagues and manager.

4. GROW YOUR OWN

There are times when it is advisable to recruit from outside the organization in order to bring in "new blood" and ideas.

Every new person who joins an organization has to be inducted into its culture and practices. It may be much more cost-effective to nurture and grow existing employees. Such people already understand the organization and its culture and objectives.

By providing opportunities for advancement to existing employees through the medium of training and development, the organization is sending out a message that it values its human capital.

Investing in the training and development of staff is a major contributor to engendering employee loyalty.

5. DON'T TREAT TRAINING AS A PUNISHMENT

If a person perceives that he or she is being trained only because of failings at work, training will be seen as a punishment. It may well be that training is needed to rectify mistakes, but a much more positive spin can be placed on it. The person is being trained not because he or she is no good but because the organization believes that the individual has potential that is not being used owing to a lack of training for the current tasks.

If the earlier point about involving people in their training has been taken on board, then the individual can be approached and asked "Is there any training that could help prevent this happening again?" In this way a dialogue will be opened that may well lead to the individual proposing a solution.

All too often mistakes and errors occur because a person was not given adequate training in the task. Questions need to be asked about why the proper training was not provided in the first place.

6. USE LEARNING STYLES TO ENHANCE THE TRAINING AND DEVELOPMENT PROCESS

The learning cycle and learning styles discussed in Chapter 6 are not just theoretical constructs but were devised from observation of people going through the learning process.

If training and development takes a person's preferred learning style into consideration wherever practicable, the effectiveness of the training will be maximized. There are questionnaires that allow trainers to ascertain an individual's preferred style. If these are used then the point at which the learning cycle is entered can be adjusted to the individual trainee. If the person is an "activist" and if there will be no damage or danger from letting the person have an initial "hands-on" with the task before looking at the instructions, then use the fact that this is the person's preferred style. If for safety reasons the individual needs a thorough grounding in the instructions before experiencing the task, then this should be pointed out. If people know why they are being trained in a particular manner or order then they will usually respond positively.

7. PUT A MONITORING AND EVALUATION PROCEDURE IN PLACE

In order to assess the effectiveness of any training and development, the success criteria need to be in place before the activities start. Learners need answers to the questions "How did I do?" "Am I on the right track?" etc.

The objectives for any training and development program should be laid out clearly in SMART criteria before any training or development activities commence. SMART criteria are:

» Specific
» Measurable
» Agreed
» Realistic
» Timebound.

8. REMEMBER THAT LEARNING NEVER STOPS

Formal learning may finish in our late teens or early 20s, but the learning process does not stop there. People still continue to learn new facts and new skills.

There are a huge number of senior citizens across the world who have developed computer skills long after they finished work. The oldest graduate (to date) of the UK's Open University was a 94-year-old lady.

You can teach an old dog new tricks if you teach them properly. Many of the senior citizens who undertook computer training did so to acquire the e-mail skills they needed to keep in touch with family members.

It is said that a person learns at least 80% of what they will ever know (including their native language) by the age of 5 years. A great deal of the remaining 20% is learnt when the person begins work and has an economic as well as a social relationship with others.

Learning organizations capitalize on the fact that as the individual employees learn so does the organization – its intellectual capital increases.

Given that learning goes on and on, it is also important that those who are approaching retirement pass on some of their skills and knowledge to juniors – this was the great strength of the apprenticeship system as it allowed skills and knowledge to be retained within the organization.

9. STRUCTURE THE TRAINING

It is a fact that people like structure. Structured tasks are much easier than unstructured ones. Tell somebody "Take as long as necessary" and the chances are they will still ask "When do you want it for really?"

Structure is what allows us to function as members of a society. Training and development also need to be structured and not undertaken in a haphazard manner.

A number of years ago the teachers in a UK city were allowed to choose from any three courses in a handbook that was produced at the beginning of the Fall semester (the "autumn term" in British education). They could choose what they wanted with no requirement for the courses to follow each other in a logical progression or to fit into their school's objectives. The courses were always over-subscribed if they took place during the school day and under-subscribed if they were in the evening or during the school vacations. A great deal about the perceived value of the courses to many of the teachers can be inferred from that – they were, for many, a day off.

Consider the European Computer Driving License described in Chapter 6 – that is a clearly structured course with a logical progression from one subject to the next and all the time building upon the skills from the previous sections.

10. DO NOT TRY TO IMPOSE DEVELOPMENT

One can impose training if really necessary but it is always best to avoid imposing such activities if the trainee is to be motivated positively.

Development can never be imposed. Development is more than learning new skills as it involves changing attitudes and often challenging one's own beliefs. Individuals have to want to be developed, as they have to engage completely with the process.

A manager may think that a person is ready for development, but the manager may have to undertake considerable groundwork with the individual. The request and the desire for development must always come from the individual and not his or her manager or anybody else in the organization. Others can sew the seeds of the idea, but in the end development is a highly personal thing.

Frequently Asked Questions (FAQs)

Q1: Isn't training and development a drain on an organization's resources?

A: There is a cost in time and money to any training or development. This should not be seen as a drain on the organization's resources, rather as an investment in its human and intellectual capital. Read about this in Chapters 1 and 2.

Q2: If I spend money training my staff won't my competitors want to entice them away?

A: The honest answer is "yes". Whether they go to a competitor or not depends on how they feel you value them in both money and personal terms. Organizations that try to grow by poaching staff from others rather than developing their own tend not to engender staff loyalty. Even if some people do leave, organizations with a good record of training and development tend to attract higher quality applicants than those that do not invest in their people. The case study of Unipart in Chapter 7 is relevant to this issue.

Q3: What is the difference between training and development?

A: Training is short-term and deals with the acquisition of a specific skill or skills. Development involves a person moving forward with their ideas and attitudes and is longer-term. The differences between training and development are considered in Chapter 2.

Q4: Why shouldn't a person's line manager be his or her mentor as well?

A: People develop a close personal relationship with their mentor. The mentor needs to be in a position to assist the individual in gaining resources to aid his or her development. There are personal and work issues that it may be inappropriate to discuss with one's manager. A good example is a mistake that the person has made but has learnt from. While the manager may well need to know about it, the ability to discuss it confidentially with somebody more experienced may well be of benefit in the person's development. Mentoring is discussed in Chapter 6.

Q5: How can training needs be assessed?

A: Training needs represent the skills gap between the skills that a person has and the skills that are needed. In times of rapid technological change skills may well become obsolete. Training needs can be identified by considering what skills are going to be needed in the future and how many of them are currently present. Training needs are discussed in Chapter 6.

Q6: What is meant by a competency?

A: A competency is a standard to which a task should be completed and is comprised of what the person needs to do, the range of activities across which he or she can do it, and the knowledge and understanding relating to the task. Competencies are covered in Chapter 6.

Q7: Why should training and development be linked to the organization's objectives?

A: If the objectives for training and development are not linked to the organization's objectives then it is pertinent to ask why the activities are taking place at all. Training and development cost time and money and thus need to add to the intellectual capital of the organization. They can do this only if they are linked to the organization's objectives. Training and development are one of the ways in which an organization achieves its objectives. Read more about the linking of training and development objectives to the organization's objectives in Chapter 6.

Q8: Must training and development always be carried out in a classroom environment?

A: Some training and development may take place in a classroom situation but the trend is towards training in the workplace. Even if training occurs out of the workplace, most learning will occur there. The Unipart "Faculty on the Floor" initiative described in Chapter 7 is an excellent example of this.

Q9: When should training and development start?

A: Training should start before a new task or procedure is introduced. It is too late to start training after its introduction. Development should begin when the individual wants it and his or her manager feels that it is appropriate. This is discussed in Chapter 10.

Q10: Where can I find out about resources to assist in training and development?

A: Lists of books, serials, and Web addresses appear in Chapter 9. There are also other titles in the ExpressExec series that are dedicated to various facets of training and development.

Index

action learning   58-9, 86, 91-2
activists   55-6
age, cultural issue   37
agreed objectives   53
American Management Association
   (AMA)   96
apprenticeships   15-16
assets, intangible   6, 44, 87
attitudes   2, 10, 36-8

behavior   7, 14, 89-90
benefits, training   49
books   96-9
British Airways case study   39-44

CAL see computer-assisted learning
Canon case study   82-4
case studies
   British Airways   39-44
   Canon   82-4
   European Computer Driving
      License   63-4
   Rosie the Riveter   70-77
   TCM.com Inc.   31-3
   Unipart   77-82
CBT see computer-based training
change   6-7, 60

coaching   10-11, 59, 86, 90
colleges   20-21
communication see information and
   communication technology
competency   63-4, 86, 112
competitive advantage   2, 3, 78
compulsory education   17
computer-assisted learning (CAL)
   27, 86
computer-based training (CBT)   27,
   86
computers
   see also information and
      communication technology
   European Computer Driving
      License   63-4
   simulations   27-8
concepts   86-93
contextualized training   52-3
continuous professional development
   (CPD)   22, 40-44, 86
costs   2, 29, 49, 111
CPD see continuous professional
   development
craftsmen   15
culture
   definition   36, 86

culture (*continued*)
  learning organizations   65
  training implications   36–48
customer capital   6

Davies, Christopher   38
definitions   6–11, 36, 86–7
development
  definition   10, 86
  models   61–2
distance learning   28, 29–30
  see also information and
    communication technology
diversity, staff   40

e-learning   22, 27–30, 31–3
  see also information and
    communication technology
ECDL *see* European Computer
  Driving License
education   10, 14, 16–21, 37, 86
effectiveness   3, 9–10, 108–9
environment   82–3
equal opportunities   37
European Computer Driving License
  (ECDL) case study   63–4, 86
evaluation   59–60, 108–9
experience   10, 37
experiential learning   58, 92

"Faculty on the Floor"   81
failure   54
FAQs *see* frequently asked questions
feedback   28
flexibility   27–9, 60, 80
formal education   14, 16–18
FOS *see* Fundamentals of
  Supervision
frequently asked questions (FAQs)
  111–13
Fry, Roger   54–5

Fundamentals of Supervision (FOS)
  40–44
further education   21

gender   37
globalization   35–45
glossary   86–8
goals   60
grudge purchases   2, 86
guilds   15

Herzberg, Frederick   2
hierarchies   36, 37
higher education   19–21
home working   30, 86
Honey, Peter   55–8, 88
human capital   6, 87
human contact   28–30
human resource management   38–9

ICT *see* information and
  communication technology
idioms   38
implementation, training   53–9
in-house training   21–2
industrial revolution   15–16
information and communication
  technology (ICT)   25–33, 87
  case study   31–3
  home working   30
  training delivery   22, 27–30,
    79–80
  user training   26, 63–4
intangible assets   6, 44, 87
integration, training and development
  78–81
intellectual capital   6, 87, 109
international issues   35–45
Internet *see* information and
  communication technology
investment   2, 42, 78–9, 106
Irving, Clive   6

Jones, Dan   78
journals   99-104
Joynt, Pat   38
just in time   80

key aspects
    concepts   86-93
    frequently asked questions
        111-13
    glossary   86-8
    resources   95-104
    ten steps   105-10
    thinkers   88-93
Klein, Peter   65-7, 88-9
knowledge   11, 14, 22
Kolb, David   54-5, 89-90

language   37-8
learning   7-9
    see also information and
        communication technology
    definition   7, 87
    experiential   92
    lifelong   28, 109
    styles   22, 55-8, 108
learning curve   7-8, 87
learning cycle   54-5, 57, 87, 89
learning organizations   64-7
Liberty ships   72-5
lifelong learning   28, 109
Logan, David   58, 90

manager-coaches   59, 90
managers, development   62, 107
Maslow, Abraham   14
Mayo, Andrew   6, 60, 61, 90-91
measurement
    development   11
    effectiveness   9-10
    objectives   53
    success   60
Mechanics' Institutes   18-19

mentoring   11, 62-3, 87, 112
models, development   61-2
monitoring   59-60, 108-9
Morton, Bob   38
motivation   2, 29-30, 54, 70-7
multi-skilling   60
Mumford, Alan   55-8, 91

needs, training   50-51, 88, 106-7,
    112
Nicholson, Mark   14

objectives
    organizations   48, 106, 112-13
    training   53
on-the-job training   51, 71-2, 74, 81
Open University (OU)   21, 29
organizations
    behavior   89-90
    flexibility   60
    global operations   36-44
    learning   64-7
    objectives   48, 106, 112-13
    standpoints   2
OU see Open University
outputs, effectiveness measure   3

partnerships, training   40-41, 80
Pettinger, Richard   60
planning, training   51-3
polytechnics   21
pragmatists   56-7
providers, training   51-3
punishment   9, 48, 107-8

quality circles   79, 91

realism, training objectives   53
recognition
    motivator   2, 49
    training importance   43-4, 78, 79
reflectors   56
research, Internet   29

resources   65-6, 95-104
Revans, Reg   58, 91-2
rewards   9, 48, 65
risk-taking   65
Rogers, Carl Ranson   58, 92-3
Rosie the Riveter case study   70-77

sandwich courses   21
Saunders, Bernard   65-7, 93
schools   16-17, 26
self-actualization   14
self-help groups   29, 65-6
serials   99-104
shipbuilding industry case study
   70-77
simulators   27-8
skills   10-11, 26, 60, 80
skills gap   51-2, 87
SMART criteria   53, 108-9
social behavior   14
specificity, training objectives   53
SS Normandie   70-72
Stauffer, David   26
Stewart, Jim   29, 58
structural capital   6
structured training   109-10
styles, learning   22, 55-8, 87, 108
success
   motivator   54
   stories   69-84
synergy   87

TCM.com Inc. case study   31-3
technology
   see also information and
      communication technology
   education   20
   environmental issues   83

telecottages   30, 87
theorists   56
thinkers   88-93
time bound objectives   53
timing, training   113
TNA *see* training needs analysis
trades, apprenticeships   15-16
training
   cycle   49-50, 87-8
   definition   9-10, 87
training needs analysis (TNA)
   48-51, 88, 112

UHI *see* University of the Highlands
   and Islands
Unipart case study   77-82
universal education   14, 16-18
universities   19-21
   distance learning   28, 29-30
   Unipart U   78-81
University of the Highlands and
   Islands (UHI)   28, 30
USS Lafayette   71-2

Victory ships   72-5
video-conferencing   28
Virtual U   79-80
vision   66
vocational training   18-19

Websites   104
Winter, Rosemary   29, 58
work-based training   14-16, 17-18,
   81
World Wide Web (WWW) *see*
   information and communication
   technology; Websites

EXPRESSEXEC –
BUSINESS THINKING AT YOUR FINGERTIPS

ExpressExec is a 12-module resource with 10 titles in each module. Combined they form a complete resource of current business practice. Each title enables the reader to quickly understand the key concepts and models driving management thinking today.

Innovation

01.01 *Innovation Express*
01.02 *Global Innovation*
01.03 *E-Innovation*
01.04 *Creativity*
01.05 *Technology Leaders*
01.06 *Intellectual Capital*
01.07 *The Innovative Individual*
01.08 *Taking Ideas to Market*
01.09 *Creating an Innovative Culture*
01.10 *Managing Intellectual Property*

Enterprise

02.01 *Enterprise Express*
02.02 *Going Global*
02.03 *E-Business*
02.04 *Corporate Venturing*
02.05 *Angel Capital*
02.06 *Managing Growth*
02.07 *Exit Strategies*
02.08 *The Entrepreneurial Individual*
02.09 *Business Planning*
02.10 *Creating the Entrepreneurial Organization*

Strategy

03.01 *Strategy Express*
03.02 *Global Strategy*
03.03 *E-Strategy*
03.04 *The Vision Thing*
03.05 *Strategies for Hypergrowth*
03.06 *Complexity and Paradox*
03.07 *The New Corporate Strategy*
03.08 *Balanced Scorecard*
03.09 *Competitive Intelligence*
03.10 *Future Proofing*

Marketing

04.01 *Marketing Express*
04.02 *Global Marketing*
04.03 *E-Marketing*
04.04 *Customer Relationship Management*
04.05 *Reputation Management*
04.06 *Sales Promotion*
04.07 *Channel Management*
04.08 *Branding*
04.09 *Market Research*
04.10 *Sales Management*

Finance

05.01 *Finance Express*
05.02 *Global Finance*
05.03 *E-Finance*
05.04 *Investment Appraisal*
05.05 *Understanding Accounts*
05.06 *Shareholder Value*
05.07 *Valuation*
05.08 *Strategic Cash Flow Management*
05.09 *Mergers and Acquisitions*
05.10 *Risk Management*

Operations and Technology

06.01 *Operations and Technology Express*
06.02 *Operating Globally*
06.03 *E-Processes*
06.04 *Supply Chain Management*
06.05 *Crisis Management*
06.06 *Project Management*
06.07 *Managing Quality*
06.08 *Managing Technology*
06.09 *Measurement and Internal Audit*
06.10 *Making Partnerships Work*

Organizations

07.01 *Organizations Express*
07.02 *Global Organizations*
07.03 *Virtual and Networked Organizations*
07.04 *Culture*
07.05 *Knowledge Management*
07.06 *Organizational Change*
07.07 *Organizational Models*
07.08 *Value-led Organizations*
07.09 *The Learning Organization*
07.10 *Organizational Behavior*

Leadership

08.01 *Leadership Express*
08.02 *Global Leadership*
08.03 *E-Leaders*
08.04 *Leadership Styles*
08.05 *Negotiating*
08.06 *Leading Change*
08.07 *Decision Making*
08.08 *Communication*
08.09 *Coaching and Mentoring*
08.10 *Empowerment*

People

09.01 *People Express*
09.02 *Global HR*
09.03 *E-People*
09.04 *Recruiting and Retaining People*
09.05 *Teamworking*
09.06 *Managing Diversity*
09.07 *Motivation*
09.08 *Managing the Flexible Workforce*
09.09 *Performance and Reward Management*
09.10 *Training and Development*

Life and Work

10.01 *Life and Work Express*
10.02 *Working Globally*
10.03 *Career Management*
10.04 *Travel*
10.05 *Flexible and Virtual Working*
10.06 *Lifelong Learning*
10.07 *Body Care*
10.08 *Free Agency*
10.09 *Time Management*
10.10 *Stress Management*

Training and Development

11.01 *Training and Development Express*
11.02 *Global Training and Development*
11.03 *E-Training and Development*
11.04 *Boardroom Education*
11.05 *Management Development*
11.06 *Developing Teams*
11.07 *Managing Talent*
11.08 *Developing and Implementing a Training and Development Strategy*
11.09 *Developing the Individual*
11.10 *Managing Training and Development Finance*

Sales

12.01 *Sales Express*
12.02 *Global Sales*
12.03 *E-Sales*
12.04 *Complex Sales*
12.05 *Account Management*
12.06 *Selling Services*
12.07 *Sales Rewards and Incentives*
12.08 *FMCG Selling*
12.09 *Customer Relationships*
12.10 *Self Development for Sales People*

Available from:
www.expressexec.com

Customer Service Department
John Wiley & Sons Ltd
Southern Cross Trading Estate
1 Oldlands Way, Bognor Regis
West Sussex, PO22 9SA
Tel: +44(0)1243 843 294
Fax: +44(0)1243 843 303
Email: cs-books@wiley.co.uk

Printed and bound by CPI Group (UK) Ltd, Croydon, CR0 4YY

13/04/2025

14656565-0003